THE ART AND SCIENCE OF MODERN TATTOOING

©ERICK ALAYØN 2004
WWW.EROCKTATTOO.COM
WWW.MODERNTATTOOSCIENCE.COM

NEW EDITION - FIRST PRINTING 2004

LIBRARY OF CONGRESS - REGISTER
1-061-773

The author has made every effort to ensure that all the information contained in this book is accurate. The author cannot accept liability for any resulting injury, damage or loss to persons or property as a result of using any of the information contained herein. Before you begin a Tattooing project, you should know how to use all of your tools and equipment safely and that you are sure and confident about what you are doing.

FOR MY CHILDREN, CHRISTOPHER AND LARA AND OUR NEW BABY, LEAH.

"OUR CHILDREN ARE THE MOST PRECIOUS GIFT THIS WORLD HAS TO OFFER. THEY LOVE US WITH AN UNCONDITIONAL LOVE THAT ONLY A CHILD CAN GIVE, THEY PRESS US TO CONTINUE WHEN THE WORLD WOULD RATHER US STAND STILL, AND THEY INSPIRE US WITH NOTHING MORE THAN A SMILE."

ERICK ALAYØN

Acknowledgments

A special thanks goes to Renee Zuppardo for proof reading and not calling me an Idiot. Northvegr, The Northern Way at www.northvegr.org. Ken Kelly, for the cool projector and all the kind words. Dana Montalto for working with me, and all the other Tattoo Artists that helped me along the way, but I can't seem to think of anyone.

And a new thanks goes to Wes from Unimax.

"TYRANNY OF ANY FORM MUST ALWAYS BE SUPPRESSED. IF A MAN CANNOT SPEAK HIS MIND ON ANY SUBJECT, THEN HE IS NOT FREE— HE IS A SLAVE TO AN OPPRESSIVE SYSTEM AND LESS THAN A MAN IF HE DOES NOT STAND BY HIS CONVICTIONS."

RON MCVAN
TEMPLE OF WOTON

•TABLE OF CONTENTS

I. TATTOOING BASICS

TUBES AND GRIPS

NEEDLES

INK

II. THE TATTOOING PROCESS

III. PRINCIPLES OF COLOR

IV. APPRENTICE INFORMATION

V. PERTINENT INFORMATION

•INTRODUCTION

This book started out as notes on tattoo machines that I just wanted to keep available, should I need to refer to them. I also figured that I could give this organized reference material to my son, when he is old enough to learn how to tattoo, if he wants to learn. I realize that while this information is out there, its not readily available, or even compiled in a single volume. It's milked out slowly, if at all, and it's hard to come by.

This is not really a how-to book, it's more like a reference guide. It is meant for a working apprentice or an experienced artist that just wants this information at his fingertips. Or for the individual that is just interested in tattooing and wants to learn a little bit about it. I don't mind sharing this knowledge with these people, in my religion selfishness, greed and cowardice are all one and the same. I'm not afraid that someone is going to learn a "tattoo secret". I once heard a saying, "A book, a cook doesn't make", and this applies to tattooing as well. I've read every book on Boat building that's out there, this doesn't mean I'm going to build a 40-foot yacht. The 14-foot beach boat I'm trying to build is giving me enough trouble! Tattooing takes practice, determination and years of hard work. It's an on going process, there is always something new to learn, and you never stop learning. And if you do stop learning, its time to pack up your shit and go home, you did it, your done, congratulations!

An experienced artist might find some of the section on the Tattooing Process basic. This section is meant for the people who don't know anything about tattooing, but get tattooed. I think they should have an understanding of whats involved in the procedure. This section may also help the budding apprentice. I hope that it does. I remember what it was like for me when I started, so I know how hard it is to get real good, solid information on tattooing. But for the ones out there that don't like to share, don't worry, there are other parts in here that will confuse the shit out of those that don't tattoo at all. These are the things that only the working Artist or Apprentice needs to know. Like the Machine section, a tattoo collector doesn't need to know a springs working length, or why a brass machine has a yoke, or what a yoke is for that matter. But knowledge should be shared. In Alexander's Great Library, the authors of the manuscripts within didn't write them for financial gain, nor was there was any such thing as a copyright. They wrote about their discoveries and adventures to share their knowledge with others, and to contribute to future generations. There is nothing wrong with you, the collector, knowing any of this information that follows. This doesn't mean that you should question your artist or act like a know-it-all. That's not what is intended, what is intended is that you know, and know quietly. I learned long ago that if you keep quiet, people will think your stupid, but when you talk, they'll know your stupid.

Well I can go on here forever, I like to talk, even if people know I'm stupid. I'll let you go, so you can get to the good stuff.

.....hold on, there's something else I have to say. When others see this book, most will ask where you got it, so they can get a copy also, by all means let them know! But a few will want you to make a copy for them, or ask if they can copy it. Please, do me a favor and don't do it. Why should they get a free copy, when you had to pay for yours? They're not special. Don't worry about being "un-cool" to them if you say no. The one who wants you to make them a free-be, ghetto-copy, is the "dick" who lacks self-respect. I've spent a lot of time and money writing and researching for this book. Not to mention printing, marketing, websites and so on, to get this book in your hands. And you've spent some time and money acquiring it. And I feel that I am asking a very fair and affordable price for this book, so it is accessible to most everyone. So please, don't let some conniving fool take the easy way out. Let them buy a copy, just like you did.

•INTRO TO THE NEW EDITION

The first edition of my book sold very well, and everyone that read it said it was great. Well, actually I didn't hear from everyone who read it. But those who I did hear from loved it. It was the people who didn't read it that didn't like it. I know this sounds stupid, but its true. A few Tattoo Artists don't like "the idea" that I wrote this book. Its not that they don't like the book, after all, how can someone judge a book they never read. It's "the idea" that they don't like. My answer to these people has always been a mighty "Go fuck yourself". This is actually quite hard for me; I knew that I wasn't going to make a lot of people happy when I published this book. I also knew that some of the people who weren't going to be happy were Artist that I admired, the same Artists who inspired me to learn to tattoo. This would have hurt me more when I was younger, but I'm older now and I really don't give a fuck. I still admire the older generation of Tattoo Artists, but...umm...I thought I had something to say here but I guess I really don't. I like to compare this book to Mel Gibson's new movie "The Passion of the Christ". A lot of people didn't like that movie, but it was the people who never even saw it that disliked it the most, just like the ones who didn't read my book.

A short while ago I sent an e-mail to another Tattoo Artist who wrote a book on tattooing. The book he wrote is very good. I asked him if He would mind if I put his link on my website. I didn't ask him to exchange links; I asked if he cared if I put his link on my site. If he wanted to link to me it would be his prerogative. I could care less if he did or didn't. I also asked if he got any "slack" from anyone for writing his book. Would you believe he didn't even have the common decency to answer my letter? Not even a simple "NO". Someone I know, who knows him, said he doesn't like "the idea" that I wrote my book. Holy shit! Here we go again, now here is the author of a book on tattooing that does not like "the idea" that I wrote a book on tattooing. What the fuck! I guess he's just another one of those ball' less wonders.

Lets get back to this book, I added a few things since the last one. My apologies go out to the people who purchased the first edition and now purchased this one. But trade manuals are always updated and this book is meant to be a trade manual. Just keep in mind that you own the first and only printing of the first edition, in a few years you can sell it on the Internet to a collector. This edition will not be updated for a while. I'm going to leave well enough alone for a while. Maybe in a few years I'll add some new things, but for now this is it. So read it and enjoy it, and drop me a line and let me know how you liked it.
Thanks,
Erick Alayon

•A BRIEF HISTORY OF TATTOOING IN EUROPE

The oldest tattoos ever discovered are on ancient Europeans. The Ice Man was tattooed over 5000 years ago, and the Bog Man is at least 2500 years old. In fact almost every ancient body they discover in the North European bogs are tattooed. The tattooed bodies of a Scythian Horseman know as the Chieftain, and a woman who archeologists call the Ice Princess, date back to 500 BCE, and were discovered in the Pazyryk region of Siberia. The bodies were perfectly preserved in their burial mound. I'm sure if Alexander's Library weren't set on fire we would know a lot more about ancient tattooing. I'm certain that tattooing goes as far back to Atlantian and Hyperborean times.

The Romans called tattoos "Stigmata Britonum", meaning "Mark of the Britons". They came up with this name while fighting the Pictish Warriors in what is now known as England. No one really knows for sure what word the Celtic Tribes used to describe their Stigmata Britonum. The body art of the Celts most defiantly had religious meaning, and may even have been done by a priest or priestess during a religious ceremony. Some of their motifs would include Knot work, spirals, and animals such as boars, horses and birds.

After 325 CE, when the council of Nicaea invented the details of Christianity, tattooing would begin to cease throughout most of Europe. It's interesting to note that the Church would only tolerate their own people being tattooed, and would even consider Christian tattoos as good and Pagan tattoos as superstitious and evil. St. Bridget, the "Christianized" Pagan Goddess Brighid (also known in other Celtic Tribes as Brigantia and Briganda), after "blessing" a group of Celtic Warriors, she would also ask God to remove the "Evil Marks" from their bodies.

Still unconverted at this time were the Norse Germanic Tribes. The Germanic Tribes, covered most of Northern Europe. The most notorious of these people were the Vikings. The Arab, Ibn Fadlan had written about his contact with the Rus Vikings in his Risala. He is quoted to say:

§ 81. Each man has an axe, a sword, and a knife and keeps each by him at all times. The swords are broad and grooved, of Frankish sort. Every man is tattooed from fingernails to neck with dark blue trees, figures, etc.

Many of these tattoos had religious significance like their Celtic cousins. I would think that the same type of symbols found on Ancient stone monuments would be the same symbols that were tattooed on the people. The body of the Viking Warrior, King Harold, after being killed in the battle of Hastings in 1066, was identified by the name Edith that was tattooed on his chest. It's very unfortunate that hardly any written record exists about ancient Tattooing. Mostly all written records were lost on the count of mass burnings done by the Church, who wanted to erase our past history. The great epic Beowulf was one manuscript that barely survived these atrocities.

After the year 1000 CE, with the official conversion of Iceland, and after the Norman Invasion of 1066 in England, tattooing and Paganism would be pushed completely "underground" in Europe. However the Old Gods were still worshipped in Lithuania and other Baltic Countries until about 1400 CE, and I am sure that tattooing was still openly alive in this area until then. On the plus side of this religious conversion, the Irish scribes would decorate the bibles they were writing with their ancient Pagan art, it may have been their way of keeping some of the old ways alive. Luckily for them the religious leaders didn't realize that the Celtic knot work they were using to illustrate the Bibles had major Pagan significance. I am sure that the first ones to do these illustrations knew the risk involved.

Tattooing would rise up again when the Great Ships made contact with the Polynesian Tribes in the Pacific. It was still taboo to be tattooed, but at least the Church was no longer burning anyone alive at the stake for having one. These Polynesians called the process of Stigmata Britonum, "Tatau". And to make a long story short, the sailors called it Tattoo, and the name stuck.

People seem to think Europe forgot how to tattoo until this resurgence. This is not exactly so, the ancient Pagan religion did not completely die out, it was just pushed underground. And since tattooing has much significance in Paganism, it's obvious that the two survived along side one another. Only the Pagans who got tattooed were probably very few, and very brave, and they would not get a tattoo someplace obvious, for fear of being burned as a witch or devil worshipper by this new, blind religion and its weak minded practitioners. When you read or hear old stories about a witch being burned alive because she had the mark of the devil, they are more than likely referring to a tattoo with Pagan significance. And to demonstrate the hypocrisy, the Church was still tolerating their own Priests getting tattooed up until the 1700's.

I. Tattooing Basics

• MACHINES

In 1876, Thomas Edison patented the Autographic Printer, which was an electric engraving device designed to engrave hard surfaces. In 1891, Samuel O'Reilly patented a modified version of Edison's machine to enable it to be used for tattooing. To change the Machine, he modified the tube system. O'Reilly's patent is only for the tube assembly, since the rest of his machine was identical to Edison's original patent for his engraver.

• ANATOMY OF A TATTOO MACHINE

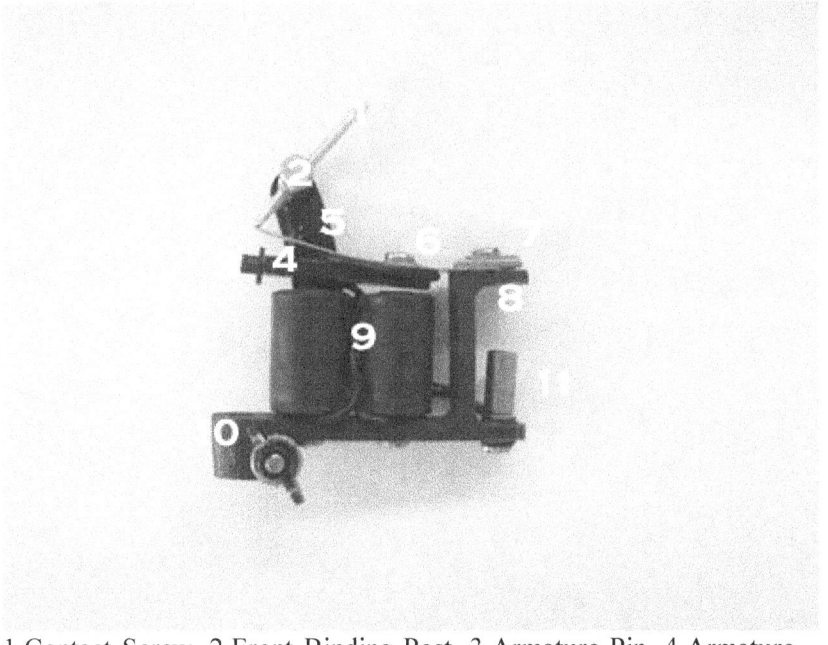

1.Contact Screw, 2.Front Binding Post, 3.Armature Pin, 4.Armature bar, 5.Forward or Front Spring, 6.Rear Spring, 7.Saddle Clamp, 8. Spring Saddle, 9. Front and Rear coils, 10. Tube Vise, 11. Rear Binding Post. Not seen is the Capacitor, which is on the right side of the machine.

•How a Tattoo Machine Works

If you look at your Machine with the clipcord attached, you will notice you have two wires hooked up, the one closest to the Spring Saddle, makes a direct connection to the Machine Frame, for this discussion we will refer to this as line #1, the Ground Line (negative). The one toward the bottom of the Frame is attached to the Rear Binding Post, this one is insulated from touching the Machine Frame. We will refer to this one as line #2, the Insulated Line (positive).

If you follow line #2, you will notice that it attaches to the capacitor and to the rear coil. The coil wire has an insulating plastic coating on it, so it won't ground out on the Frame. If you follow the capacitor up to the other end you will notice that the negative end attaches to the Front Binding Post, along with the wire that comes out of the Forward Coil.

The Front Binding Post is also insulated from touching the Machine Frame. The Front Binding Post has the Contact Screw running through it, which comes in contact with the Forward Spring. This contact screw should be made of silver, if it isn't, you should replace it.

The Forward Spring might have a Contact Point attached to it, which the Contact Screw will touch, not all Machines have this and it really isn't necessary. Now if you follow the Forward Spring toward the rear of the Machine, you will notice that the Rear Spring sits on the Spring Saddle, and since it is touching the Frame it makes a connection to line #1, to complete the circuit. The only contact between line #1 and line #2 that can be changed is where the contact point touches the Forward Spring.

If you pull the Armature bar down to touch the forward coil, you will break contact. (The Armature bar should never touch the rear coil, there should be a very small gap between them.) Now Step on the foot pedal, to run your Machine. What happens is the Coils, which are Magnetic Coils, get charged, the magnetic force pulls the Armature Bar down, which breaks the electric connection when the Forward Spring looses contact with the contact screw. This turns the Magnetic Coils off, so the Armature Bar springs back up to make another connection with the Contact Screw, which turns the Magnetic Coils back on, and starts the cycle over again.

So what we have is a machine that turns itself on and off, repeatedly. If line #2 is ground to the Frame it will cause the Magnetic Coils to remain on, which will keep the Armature Bar pulled down to the coils.

•Machine Frames

Machine Frames are usually made from Brass, Iron, or Aluminum. Some old Machines were made from a stuff called Bakelite, but these are rare and are mainly collectors' items today. Some suppliers sell Copper and Bronze Machines, but these are a bit heavy. Machines can be cast, machined, screwed or welded together. The method of construction all depends on the individual builder. Bolted or welded frame construction is usually used when the builder is building custom machines that are made to order. Builders that make a large quantity of the same frame style use machined and Cast Frames. Although this isn't always the case, as you often see large manufacturers building bolted frames, and small custom builders using cast frames.

BRASS: Brass is probably the most popular material for frames. It's a good conductor, it's got a good weight to it if you like a heavy machine, and it casts well. Most of the brass frames you see are cast.

IRON: While Brass is the most popular material among the "Old Timers", Iron, or Steel, is probably the best material for Machine Frames. It conducts better than brass and it is not as heavy. Iron Frames can be cast or made from malleable iron, which is welded, bent, forged or machined to shape.

ALUMINUM: Most people don't like aluminum, most likely because it is not a good conductor. Which means you need more power to run it at a good operating speed. On the plus side it is very strong and lightweight. As far as being a poor conductor, I think this can be used for certain advantages. I use an aluminum machine for all my black and gray work. Being a poor conductor it runs slow and hits soft, which works well for my style of black and gray. I turn the power down to hit soft for areas for lighter tones and I can turn the power up to hit harder for solid areas. Or if there is a larger area that has to be solid black, I can use one of my other machines that hit real hard. Don't limit yourself to using the traditional set-up of liner and shader. A painter uses several brushes, a Sketch Artist uses several pencils, there is no reason why you can't use more than two Machines while doing a tattoo.

• MACHINE SPRINGS

There are many deciding factors in how well a machine runs, frame material, capacitor, contact screw and springs. Of all these, the springs are the most important. Springs can be made from Feeler gauge stock or spring steel.

Springs determine the speed of the machine and how much voltage is required to achieve that speed. The Forward spring determines the speed, the thicker the forward spring the faster it will run, the thinner the forward spring the slower it will run. The Back spring provides the tension, which is how much pressure the front spring will press with against the contact screw. It too, will determine the speed of your machine.

The following is a discussion of Machine Springs. It may sound a bit confusing at first, but it really isn't that bad. You really don't have to know all of it, unless you want to build custom machines. But a basic knowledge of the variables that make a machine run fast or slow, make it hit hard or soft will help you fine tune your machine to your own particular style of Tattooing.

REAR SPRING: The Actual length of the Rear Spring should be 1 1/2". The Working Length of the Rear spring is measured from the front of the Spring Saddle to the center of the armature bar screw. The shorter the Working Length, the slower the Machine. Because of standard machine measurements, if you want to increase your spring working length you can file the top forward portion of the spring saddle at a 45° angle. The more stock you remove the longer your spring working length will be. Remember that a modification like this is irreversible. The width of Rear Spring is usually a

½ inch or ⅝ of an inch. The wider the Rear Spring is, the stiffer the tension will be, so once again this is another variable to consider. The final Rear Spring measurement is thickness. The thicker the spring the stiffer the tension, which will, as we said, soften the hit. If you want a hard-hitting machine then use a thinner Rear Spring. Another thing to remember is that a Stiff Rear Spring will slow the Machine down a little, and a Soft Rear Spring will make it run a little faster.

FORWARD SPRING: The length of the Forward Spring is about 1 5/8". About 1/2 from the rear of the spring both sides should taper forward to the front so the tip has a flat edge of about 1/8" wide. It should also bend up 1/2" from the rear at an angle of about 15°. The width of the spring should be 1/2". A thick Forward Spring will be stiff and make the Machine run faster, and a thin Forward Spring will be soft and make the Machine run slower.

A common practice is to put a rubber o-ring under the front spring and drag it over the armature screw. This makes the Machine run smoother, at least it sounds like it runs smoother. But we do use the sense of hearing while we tattoo, as well as sight and touch, so if the Machine sounds smoother it will help make our work easier. Nobody likes to tattoo with a clunky sounding Machine.

Heres a cool trick you can do to your forward spring. I have a Liner that kept crapping out on me, no matter what I did it just wouldn't run smooth. I had this Machine for years, since 1995, and I use it everyday. I would alternate the Shaders I use, but I would only line with this Machine. Now here it is giving me problems. I know that stiffer forward springs make a Machine run smoother. I also know that it will speed up the Machine, which is what I didn't want. I, strangely enough, prefer a slower running liner. One day I said "fuck it", and I doubled up the forward spring. Yeah, I stacked two springs one on top of the other and put it on the Machine, and you know what, the Machine runs so smooth now I cant believe it. And the speed isn't much of a difference that it hindered my technique. If you do this, stack two flat springs perfectly aligned. Hold them where you want the bend to be with long nose pliers and bend both of them together, so they match. Attach them to your Armature bar and let'em rip. You wont be disappointed, in fact I did this to all my Machines, but don't tell anyone about this trick, its our little secret.

SADDLE CLAMP: The saddle clamp is located on top of the rear spring. Not all Machines have a Saddle clamp and they aren't absolutely necessary. But a Saddle clamp will make a difference in the way your Machine runs.

If you pull your armature bar down by the pin you will see how the rear spring bends at the front of the spring saddle. Now if you watch the spring move back to the relaxed position it bends back up. But if you don't have a saddle clamp, the working length of the spring on the up stroke is longer than the working length on the down stroke. You have a screw and a washer holding the rear spring in place. If you measure from the front of this washer to the rear of the armature bar, this is your working length on the up stroke. If you want to examine this in the extreme, remove the front binding post and push up on your armature bar. If you look at the rear spring you will see it lifting off the spring saddle. If you do this experiment with a saddle clamp in place you will see that it evens up the working length.

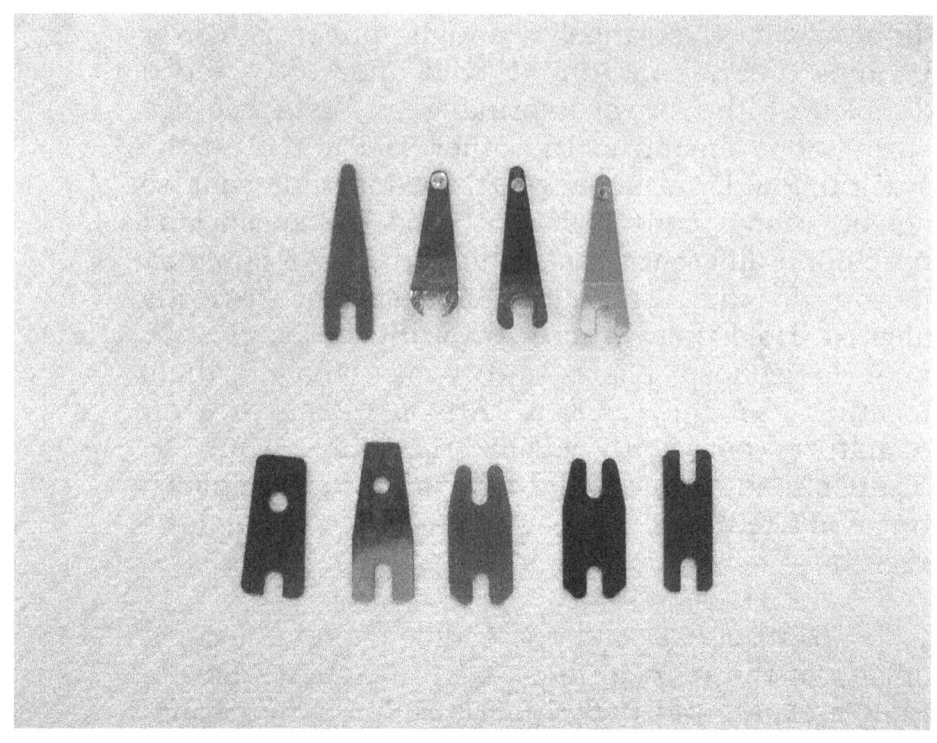

Different types of forward and rear springs.

•MACHINE COILS

Coils come in different sizes. First there are different heights. Some Machines use the shorter coils which are 1" in height, some machines use the taller ones, which are a height of 1 1/4" or 1 3/8". The way to measure the strength of the coil is by how many wraps there are, which means how many times the coil wire wraps around the coil core. The wire is either #24 or #26 insulated magnet wire. There are three common types of coils, 8 wrap, 10 wrap, and 12 wrap. Sometimes you might come across 14 wrap coils, but these are rare and usually custom made and can easily damage the skin. An experienced Tattoo Artist should only use these coils.

I mentioned that the stronger coils are the ones with the most wraps. What I mean by this is they have the potential to be stronger. Coils are electro-magnets, the more current you put through them the more magnetic power they have. The more wraps a Coil has, the more power it needs, and also the more power it can handle. If you run a Machine with 8 wrap coils at, lets say 12 volts, and run a similar Machine with 10 wrap coils at the same voltage, the 8 wrap coil will have more strength. A 12-wrap coil will be even weaker at the same current. However the 8-wrap coil will tend to get hotter quicker, whereas the 10-wrap coil will handle more current without being overloaded. This makes the larger coil more efficient. Since you can put more current through the bigger coils, they have the potential to run stronger.

Depending on what type of frame you use the coils would rest on what is called a Yoke. A Yoke is a piece of steel or iron that sits on the Frame Base and the coils sit on top of this.

The reason for a yoke is that for the coils to work properly they must form a horseshoe magnet. If the frame is made from a non-ferrous metal, like brass or aluminum, you will need a yoke. The yoke should be about the same thickness as the coil core. If you look at your Machine and picture the coil cores protruding up from the ends of the yoke, you will see a squared U shape. If the Yoke is too thin the Machine will not run right, and can even run hot. The only Machines that do not require a Yoke is an Iron Machine, all other Machine materials require the use of a Yoke.

The Armature Bar should never touch the Rear Coil when it is in the down position. It should sit flat on the top of the Front Coil, and there should be a slight space between it and the top of the Rear Coil. You can raise the coils to the proper position with the use of very thin washers called shims.

In case you haven't noticed the coil cores are drilled and tapped to secure them to the Machine. Since the coils are electro magnets you should only use steel screws to hold the coils in place, as non-ferrous screws such as brass will not magnetize and this will affect the strength of your coils. For some reason, some people drill and tap the coils real deep. This creates a hollow space at the top of the coil, where solid material is needed the most. Even if your coils were drilled and tapped right there will still be a hollow space above the screw when it is screwed in place. To fix this, hold the coil in place on the Machine and place a toothpick in the hole. Now mark the spot where the toothpick is even with the bottom of the Machine frame. From this mark to the tip that was in the coil is how long the screw should be. Get one a little shorter so there wont be a problem screwing it in. if you decide to get a longer one and cut it to size, remember to put a nut on it before you cut it. This way after you cut it, you unscrew the nut and this will fix any threads that get messed up. And if you want to fill the small space still remaining you can cram small pieces of steel wool in the coil, but don't put too much because it's a real pain to get out.

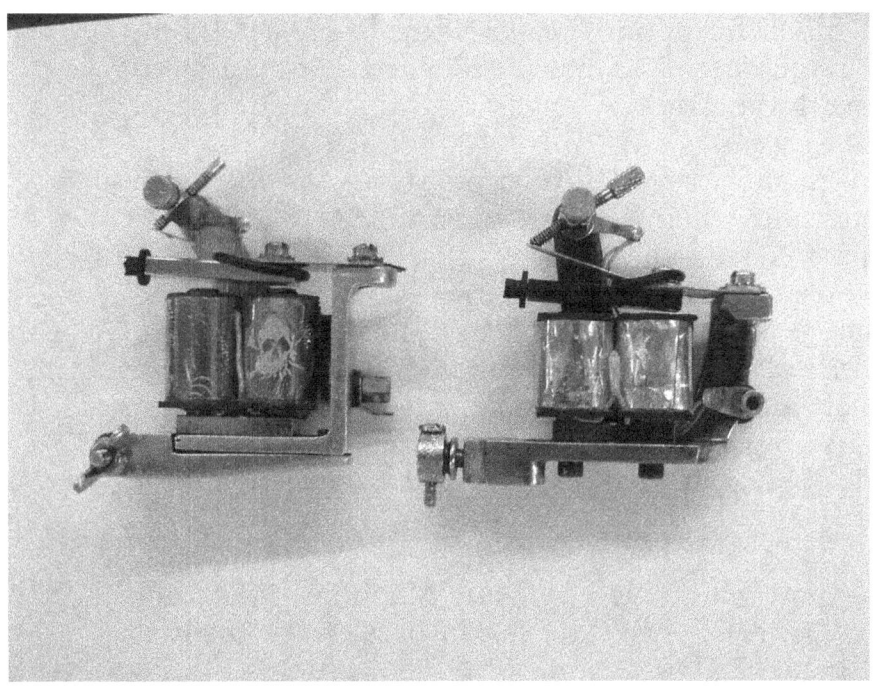

Two examples of coils seated on a yoke. An Aluminum Frame (left) and a Brass Frame (right).

8 WRAP COILS: These coils are the weakest. Some Artists like them for outlining. I don't think there are very many Professional Tattoo Artists who use 8 wrap coils these days. The problem with 8 wraps is that they get hot. Sometimes they get so hot that the Artist can't even hold the Machine. I do not recommend using 8 wrap coils at all.

10 WRAP COILS: These are the most common coils. They are good for lining or shading and coloring. Most Professional Machines you buy today come with 10 wrap coils.

12 WRAP COILS: 12 Wrap Coils are good hard-hitting coils. They are great for color Machines. I use a 12 wrap machine to outline with, which a lot of people see as a bit "different". If your ordering a shader Machine from a supplier, and they have the option for 12 wrap coils, get them. But remember 12's hit harder so it is easy to overwork the skin.

A shorter coil is not as strong as its taller counterpart when it comes to wraps. A 1" coil of 10 wraps will be weaker then a 1 1/4" 10 wrap coil, and even weaker than a 1 3/8" 10 wrap coil. The reason is kind of obvious; the taller coil has more coil wire. This is why an Iron Machine runs the best out of all the other frame materials, not just because of its conductivity, but because it does not need a Yoke it usually has the taller, strongest coils.

You will notice on your Machine Coils that the coil wire is very thin. It can break very easily if you bend it back and forth too much. If this happens you can repair it quite easily. Simply cut the Coil covering a little bit from the bottom so you can pull the wire that snapped off out. You may have to grab it with tweezers or a thick sewing needle. When you get it, unwrap the wire once around, so you have about an inch of wire. Take a small file and gently scrape away the red insulating material that the wire is coated with, and resolder it where it belongs.

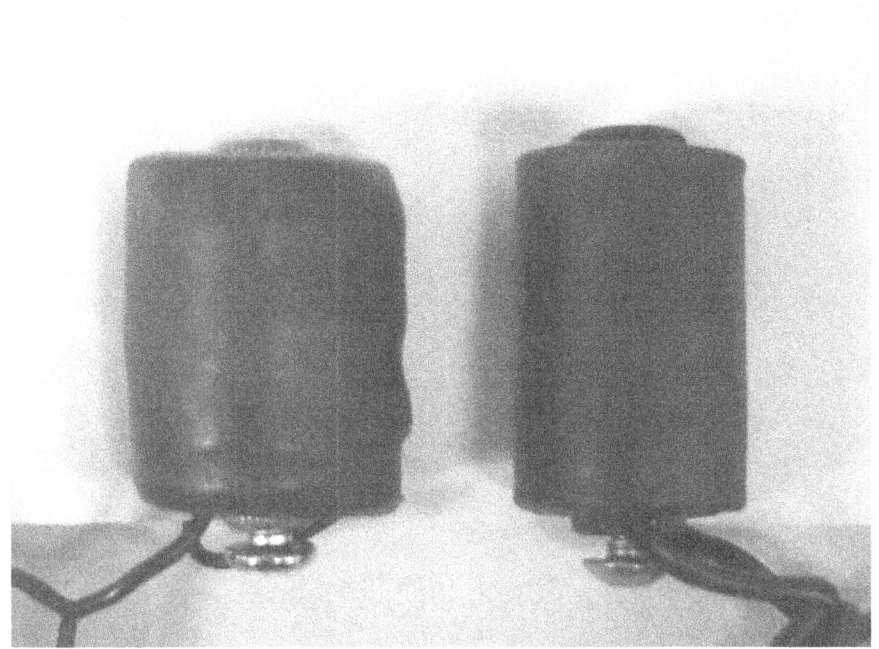

A comparison of a 14-wrap coil on the left, to a 10-wrap coil on the right.

•ARMATURE BARS

Armature bars are 3/16" thick and usually 3/8" wide, and are always made from a ferrous material because they have to be pulled down by the magnetic coils. Some suppliers sell ones that are wider. The extra width adds weight to the Armature bar. The weight of the Armature bar has a factor in the speed of the machine. A heavy weight Armature bar will move slower and hit harder than a lightweight one.

To lighten the weight of an armature bar you can grind or file some material off the top of the bar. Be sure not to file any thing off where the springs attach, this must remain the stock thickness. Start filing about a 1/2" or so from the rear of the bar so as not to ruin where the spring sits. I have also seen grooves cut into an armature bar across the width to make it lighter.

To add weight to the Armature bar you can take a nickel or a quarter, or a piece of brass and cut it to the width of the bar, which should be 3/8", and cut it to a length to meet your desired weight. This you will have to experiment with. You can temporarily stick them down with a weak adhesive to check the difference in the way the Machine runs. When you get the Machine running the way you like, you can solder the weight on to the bar. You will have to use a flame, as a conventional soldering iron will not be hot enough. You can also tap a hole and screw the weight on. The weight of the screw may even be enough. Make sure the added weight does not interfere with the forward spring. The weight should be as far forward as possible, but not protrude over the armature pin. A heavy bar would add some nice momentum for putting in color.

When adjusting an Armature bar on your machine, you have to make sure that it is centered above the tube vise. In actuality, the forward part of the Armature bar, where the pin sticks out, should be slightly off-centered to the rear, to make up for the rubber nipple or grommet that you use to dampen the needle bar. If you don't use a rubber grommet of some sort, you should. Paper or tape went out of style a long time ago, with acetate stencils.

•Capacitors

An electrical current is the flow of charged electron particles. This flow of electrons must be around a circuit, from the source, through the device and back to the source. This is how direct current (dc) works. Alternating current, known as "Mains Electricity" works a bit different. It is much more powerful, and in ac the current flows in one direction and then the opposite direction. The rate or frequency at which the current changes direction is very rapid. It is measured in Hertz. In something that is 50 Hertz (50Hz), the current cycles one way and then the other 50 times per second.

A capacitor is a device for the storage of an electric charge. A Simple capacitor consists of two plates made of an electrically conducting material and separated by a nonconducting material or dielectric such as glass, paraffin, mica, oil or paper. If voltage is applied to a capacitor, the plates will become charged, one positively and one negatively. If the externally applied voltage is then removed, the plates of the capacitor remain charged, and the presence of the electric charge induces an electrical potential between the plates. This phenomenon is called electrostatic induction. The capacity of the device for storing electric charge is its capacitance, which is measured in micro Farads, uF. The main capacitor classifications are non-polarized (used for AC circuits) and polarized (used for DC circuits). Capacitors can also be classified as fixed or variable. A type of variable capacitor was used in radio and television tuning circuits. It consisted of two sets of semicircular plates, one fixed and the other mounted on a movable shaft. By rotating the shaft the area of overlap of the two plates increases or decreases, thus increasing or decreasing the capacitance.

A Capacitor is what makes the Machine run smoothly, and reduces the spark at the contact point and front spring. With out a capacitor your Machine would spark like an Arc Welder.

To read a capacitor, look at the two numbers. The first one is the voltage rating. This is how much voltage it can take before it explodes. 25V is sufficient for a Tattoo Machine because you never run more than 12 volts thru your Machine, although some artists insist on 35V, the choice is yours. The next number is the capacity ratio, which is measured in micro Farads, this is how much electricity it can store. 22uF or 47uF are the ones most commonly used. Others work well also, you can experiment with different sizes if you get bored during the winter months. The larger capacitors will absorb more current than the smaller ones, which means the larger Capacitor you use the slower your Machine will run. Whichever size you decide to use make sure you attach it so the negative side connects with the Front Binding Post. Not every one follows this, and I don't think it really matters. But, capacitors can explode if the current runs through them the wrong way, so I guess it does matter.

If you have a Clip cord with the negative and positive marked on the wire, attach the negative to the Spring Saddle, which is, as we know the negative ground line. But if the capacitor is hooked up in reverse, meaning the negative end connected to the rear binding post, attach the negative wire to it. You may be better off resoldering the capacitor on the right way. Does the Machine run any different if its not? I don't know. If it does you can't tell with the naked eye.

•Machine Measurements

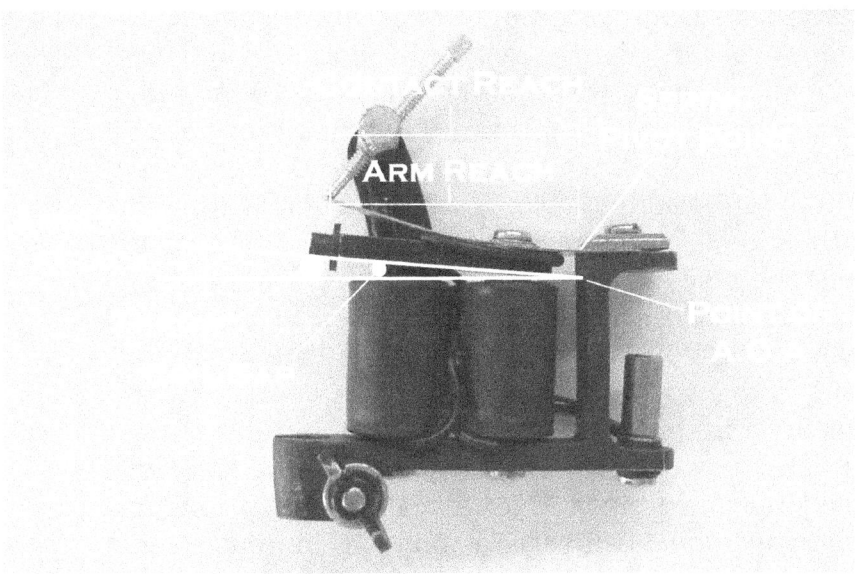

When the forward spring is touching the contact point it is in the Relaxed Position. When the armature bar is resting on the coils the machine is in the Seated Position.

CONTACT REACH: This is the measurement from the Spring Pivot Point to the tip of the contact screw. If you change the Contact Reach you affect how fast the Machine runs. The shorter the Contact reach the faster the Machine will run. Cutback liners have a small contact reach this is why they run fast. The reason the speed is affected is the front spring is stiffer the further back you go. When you have the contact point touching at the extreme end, like the Machine in the photo, the spring is softer so it will run slower. Cutback Machines also use a short Point Gap and because of the longer Arm Reach compared to the short Contact Reach the Machine has a longer Throw or Angle of Attack. Which results in penetration and speed.

43

ARM REACH: This is the measurement from the spring pivot point to the tip of the Armature bar. Don't include the nipple when you measure. If you look at the picture you will notice that the Throw will increase the further out you extend the Armature bar. Because of manufacturing standards a Machine will have to be custom built to accommodate a longer Arm Reach. As you will pass the tube vise if you extend it out too far. However if you cut the vise off your machine with a rotary tool, and add one of those replacement vises some of the suppliers sell, you can extend it out a little further. You may have to drill new holes in the replacement vise or even better, oval them to allow adjustments. If you start extending the Arm Reach out too far you will need a longer Armature bar and a longer rear spring also. This alteration will increase the Throw or Angle of Attack without adjusting rear spring tension or point gap. Please remember that once you cut your vise off that's it, it's gone forever. This doesn't matter if you have one of those older crappy vises.

ANGLE OF ATTACK: Sounds cool don't it, Angle of Attack. This is the same as Throw but it sounds more menacing. And I'm a big fan of menacing. Every thing you should know about Angle of Attack is discussed in the Arm Reach section.

SPRING PIVOT POINT: This is where the spring pivots. Usually at the front corner of the Spring Saddle. You can change the Spring Pivot Point by filing an angle on the spring saddle. If you do this you are changing the both the Contact reach and the Arm Reach. This will speed the machine up a little without changing the Angle of Attack. But remember that this is an irreversible alteration.

COIL GAP: This is the distance between the top of the forward coil to the bottom of the Armature Bar. The Coil Gap is measured either at the front or center of the forward coil core, the choice is yours. Coil Gap is not always the same as Point Gap. Because of rear spring tension, the forward spring can flex a little when it is in the relaxed position.

POINT OF A.O.A.: This is where the line of relaxed Point of Attack intersects with the line of the seated Point of Attack. This point changes if you adjust the Arm Reach by sliding the rear spring forward or backward. It really doesn't matter where it is located, I just thought you would like to know about it. :)

•TUBES AND GRIPS

•TUBES

Tubes are usually about 4 1/4" long, with an outside diameter of 5/8". Suppliers sell disposable lexan tubes, but these really suck and I never met a professional Tattoo Artist who uses them. Get stainless steel ones, they come either soldered or two piece. The Soldered tube is the length of tube with the tip crimped and soldered in place. The two-piece tube consists of a tube stem about 2 3/4" long and a machined tube tip that attaches to the stem and is held in place by the setscrews on the tube grip. The stem and the tip can be either male or female. Of course if the tube is a male then the tip will be female and vise versa.

TIPS: Tips are machined and as I said above are male or female. Most people like the female tips, as the male tips leave an edge on the inside of the tube stem. This edge can damage the needles when you slide them into the tube. To stop this you can bend the needles down a little at the end of the bar, which is what you should be doing anyway. NEVER BEND THE BAR!!! This is wrong, the needle bar should remain straight. Only bend the needles slightly. This stops the needle bar from riding on back of the tube, which will seriously affect the way the machine runs. And can also make the ink ride up the bar to the top of the tube and make mess. I've seen it happen, and it's not a pretty sight. Anyway, when your inserting the needle bar in the tube, with the needles bent slightly down, ride the bar flat on the inside top of the tube. By doing this, the tips of the needles will be traveling down the middle of the tube and pass right thru the center of the notorious tip edge, and make it thru completely unscathed. If your needles are bent too much, they will either scrape on the inside bottom of the tube or hit against the bottom of the tip edge.

•GRIPS

Grips are made from stainless steel, nylon, brass or aluminum, and range in diameter from 1/2", which is pretty much extinct now, up to 1" and sometimes even larger. The larger the grip the better, because by using a thin grip you can develop hand problems like carpel tunnel. The larger the grip the easier it is on your hand. I use a 1" grip, they take a little getting used to when you first start using them but after you get used to them you will never go back to thin grips. Nylon and aluminum grips are lightweight and some artists prefer them over the other materials when using the fatter grips. I like the stainless steel ones as they are heavier and act as a counter balance to the machine. When I use the nylon grip on the machine it feels a little top heavy.

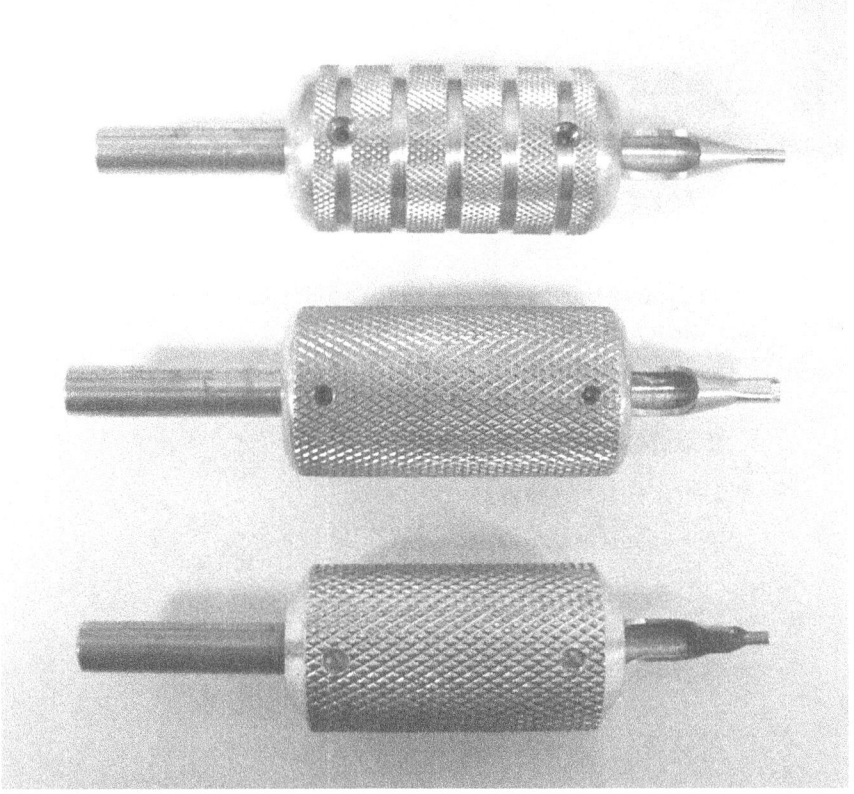

Tubes with different style 1" grips. On the Top is a 2-piece liner. In the Center is a 2-piece shader. On the Bottom is a 1-piece soldered tip liner.

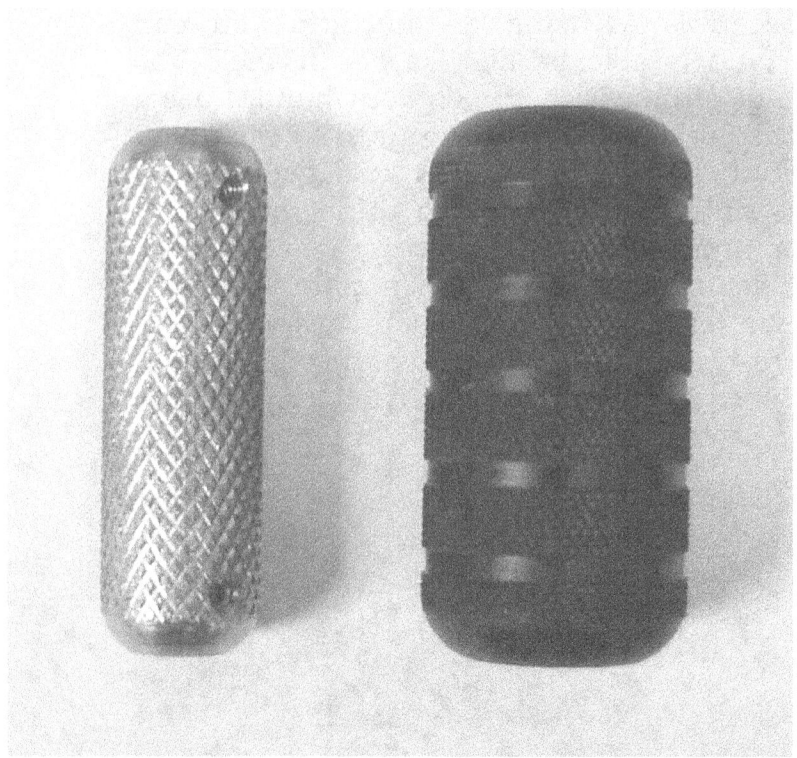

Two more different types of grips. On the Left is 5/8" stainless steel grip. On the Right is a 1" lightweight nylon grip.

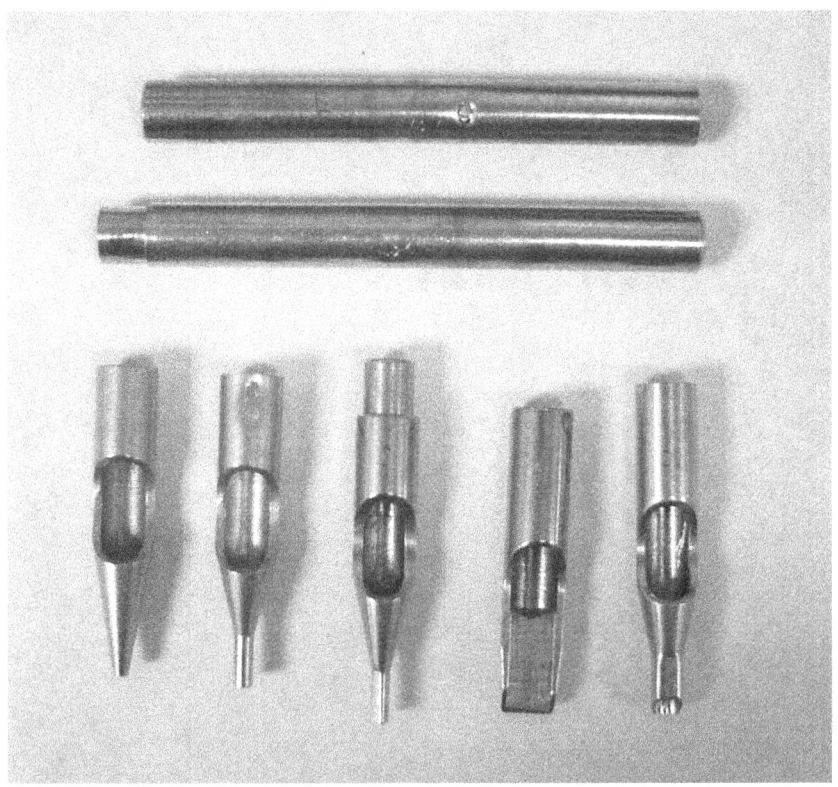

Tube stems with various tube tips. On top is a female stem. Under this one is a male stem. The tips from left to right is a f-liner, another f-liner, m-square tip liner, f-shovel tip   shader, f- square shader tip.

•NEEDLES

There are a few different kinds of needles you should be familiar with. They are Long Taper #12, Short Taper #12, and Insect Pins, also known as Bug Pins. You can also get the long and short taper needles in #10 size. I don't use these so I can't give any information on them, but it would seem they are good for coloring because of the extra thickness. Needles can be made from stainless steel or carbon steel.

•SHADERS

Although these are called Shaders, and the Machine you use them in is called the Shader Machine, they are used for Shading and Coloring. Carbon steel needles are the best for doing color work. The reason for this is that they are not smooth. If you look at them under a powerful microscope you will see small pits. This is beneficial in that these pits hold the pigment when the needle enters the skin. The skin then hugs the needle as it pulls its way out, holding the pigment in the skin. Stainless needles are smooth, so when the needle enters the skin and pushes thru, the hugging skin pushes the ink up before it can enter the skin. This is not to say that Tattoos can't be done with Stainless Steel Needles, the majority of them are done this way, it's just that Carbon Needles get more ink in the skin in a single pass.

The draw back of Carbon Needles is that they rust very quickly. This means you should make them just prior to using them. An old fashioned way of keeping them from rusting is after making them, clean them good, sterilize them, and right from the sterilizer stick them needle first into a tub of petroleum jelly. They will remain sterile. But in these modern times this is against Board of Health Practice, and most customers want to see their needles come out of sterilized pouches.

Short taper stainless steel needles are the next best thing for doing color work. If you look at short taper needles thru an eye loop, you will see that they taper down to a point kind of like a bullet does. Because of this steep taper they stretch the skin more than the long taper at a shallower penetration, this allows more color pigment to enter the skin with less trauma. And being made from stainless steel, they don't rust.

Most Artists I know don't make their needles, they buy them pre-made from a supplier. There is nothing wrong with this practice. A Tattoo Artist puts in very long hours at the Tattoo Shop and the last thing they want to do when they go home is make needles. And it's usually too busy to make needles in the shop, and if its not busy, you don't need any needles anyway.

Time at home is better spent with your family. I'm sure you wife and children would rather see you enjoying this time with them, instead of making needles. Cursing every five minutes because you burnt your finger on the soldering iron, and tasting flux on your sandwich because you didn't wash it all off you fingers good enough, if you even washed your hands at all.

Buy your needles pre-made, unless you insist on using the carbon ones, or the insect pins. Some places sell needles made from bug pins. A 9 needle Magnum made from 00 insect pins is the best needle for doing Black and Gray. If ever there was a Tattoo Secret, this is it. A 9 magnum made from 00 insect pins will fit in a regular 7-needle magnum tube, because the 00's are thinner than the standard #12 needles. And because they are thinner, when you use them for gray wash shading, the grays look smoother than if you used standard #12's. If you do or plan on doing portraits or other major Black and gray work, you should buy and get used to using 9 needle 00 Magnums made from bug pins.

With all this talk about Magnums I think I should tell you what Magnums are. First lets start with Flats. Amateurs use flat needles. A Flat needle is just that, a row of needles, usually 4 or 6, laid out flat and soldered. These needles suck! You can't Tattoo anything with them, don't even try. They won't put ink in if Odin himself were to come down from Valhalla and try to make it work. It just won't happen.

Magnums, on the other hand, work great! A Magnum is basically a flat, most commonly a 7 needle flat, but before it is soldered down towards the tips a piece of foil or a thin razor blade is weaved between the needles. What this does is separate them so you have 4 needles on the bottom and 3 needles on the top. They alternate like a row of matches in a matchbook. They are also made with 9 needles, or 11 and so on. Always an odd number so you have one more on the bottom than on the top. These are also referred to as Woven Flats. There are also Double Stacked Magnums, which are two flats soldered one on top of the other. In this case a 7 Double Stacked Magnum would be a 3 flat soldered on top of a 4 flat. This needle will only be 4 needles wide so you would need a 4 needle square tube to use it. Double Stacks are not good for putting in color, however you get nice looking results when gray shading, comparable to the 00 Bug pins.

Some Artists might tell you that Magnums are more difficult to use than Flats. They will say that it is easier to over-work the skin with a Magnum. This is not true, it's easier to over-work the skin with a flat because a flat just does not work. And an artist using a flat will keep trying to put ink in the same spot, over and over and over, see what's happening, your over working the skin. A magnum puts the ink in right away, there's no need to go over the spot again and again, one pass is all it takes, two if your client is a bleeder. If you plan on making Magnums, but don't have the proper instruction on how to do it, or if you suspect that you weren't taught the right way, buy a few from a supplier. This way you can see how they are made, and how they should look.

It is good to know how to make your own needles, and also to have experience in making needles. But when all that is said and done, and you want to have a life and live it too, buy your needles. There are plenty of good suppliers out there selling pre-made needles, and their business is booming.

• LINERS

Long taper needles are for outlining, you can tighten the group to a nice point, but don't make it too tight, you need it to be able to hold ink, otherwise you will get a real crappy line. The most common liners are single, 3, 5, and 7. And come in loose or tight configuration. They are usually referred to as Rounds. The ones you buy from a supplier will be kind of in between tight and loose. I also like to use 4's, and some artists use 8's and 10's or more. In the following discussion you will notice I use the term Calligraphy, or Calligraphied Line. A Calligraphied Line is a line that is intentionally done with thick and thin areas. As if you did it with a calligraphy pen. A good example of this is the old 1950's advertising illustration.

SINGLE NEEDLE: This is the famous Fine Line needle. As its name implies it is only a single. A single working needle that is, actually it is comprised of 3 needles in a triangle shape, with two of the needles pulled back far enough so they don't penetrate the skin. These are known as feeder needles, because it is said they hold the ink to feed to the working needle. They actually serve to strengthen the single needle. Singles are very unforgiving, any slightest wobble will be seen in the finished piece. These are only good for doing very thin lines, with no calligraphy. Although a lot of Tattoo Artists do single needle work, there are very few good single needle Tattoo Artists around. The key to being a good Tattoo Artist is knowing your limitations.

3 NEEDLE: 3 needle liners make a nice thin line, but not as thin as a single needle, they are a little more forgiving. 3's are good for that small rose or butterfly. They are also good to do calligraphied lines on these smaller pieces.

4 Needle: These are the needles you have a love hate relationship with. A liner is also called a Round, because the configuration is always more or less round. But this is not so with a 4, 4's are square; you can't make them round. Because of this it's difficult to get a smooth edge line. The reason for this is that since the 4 needles form the shape of a square, the group is thinner from edge to edge, than it is from point to point. To see this draw a perfect square, 1 inch on each side. Now if you measure from side to side it will be 1 inch, but if you measure from corner to corner it will be about 1 7/16". That's a big difference, almost 50% bigger. So what all this comes down to is you really have no choice but to Calligraphy the lines. If you don't want Calligraphied lines, you should use the 3 or the 5 liner.

5 Needle: Some artists don't use needles any smaller than a 5. 5's are a good all around needle, and can be made tight or loose. You can get very thin lines with a tight 5, sometimes an Artist looking over your work would be surprised when he learns that you did the lining with a 5.

7 Needle: These are what to use if you're into the Old School Style of Tattooing. They make a good, solid, bold line that will last a long time. These are also good for doing those little Kanji tattoos all the girls like to get. Just fill it in solid as you go, and you can do one in less then two minutes. I once timed myself from the time the needle hit the skin to when the Kanji was finished. I dipped twice, and finished the tattoo in 45 seconds!

8 NEEDLE: These are basically 7 rounds with one needle right in the middle. What this does is give you a nice fat line, like the 7, but you don't have to worry about so much about Hollow lines. A Hollow line is when you do an outline and it is not solid in the middle. This happens when you use loose needle groups.

These are all the needles I'm going to talk about, because these are the ones I have the most experience with. If the majority of your work is going to be large, you may find yourself using 15 magnums or 12 rounds or some other big needle configuration. My basic setup is a 5 liner and a 7 magnum. For smaller tattoos I'll use a 3 liner, and on occasion I'll use a 7. If I'm doing a portrait I'll use a 00-9 Magnum, and either a 5 or a 3 liner, or both. Each Tattoo is different, you, as the Artist have to decide how you're going to do it, and what tools you will use. If you ask three Tattoo Artists how they will go about doing a particular Tattoo and what tools they will use, you will more than likely get three different answers.

•How to Make Needles

JIGS: While there are a lot of different styles of jigs on the market, there are only three types, a Grouping jig, a Needle Tightening jig, and a Needle Bar jig. The Grouping jig is used to make the needle groups, and the tightening jig is used to tighten the groups. The Bar jig is used to attach the finished groups to the bar. Some Grouping jigs are also Tightening jigs. The jigs are usually sized for #12 Sharps.

LINER GROUPS: To make a liner group simply put the required amount of needles in the proper size jig, make sure they are flush at the points and apply a little flux with a pipe cleaner and tack the ends with silver solder. Do not use solder that contains lead, as lead is toxic.

When you get a bunch of groups tacked together, flux them again, from the tack towards the tip. Don't go all the way to the tip, you don't want to bring the solder too far down. You want to do this step in the tightening jig. Carefully apply solder and drag it towards the tip. But make sure the solder does not go to the points. You want to tattoo with needle, not solder. You also have to be careful not to heat the group too much or the tack will pop under the pressure of the tightening jig.

SINGLE NEEDLE LINER: To make a single needle, make a 3 needle liner. Tack the ends as usual, but before soldering the rest of the way, snip off about ⅛" to ¼ " of two of the needles, then bring the solder down almost to the end of these. These are the feeder needles, they say that they help feed ink to the single needle. I think they really serve to help strengthen the single needle so it doesn't bend under pressure of the rubber bands when the Machine is set up.

MAGNUM GROUPS: Shader groups are much easier to make than the liner groups. Simply lay out the amount of needles for the group, we'll use 7 for this example. Make sure all the points are even, if you're using a jig you shouldn't have any problem. Tack the ends as described above. Next place a piece of foil or a thin double edged razor blade in between the needles, so you have 4 on the bottom layer and 3 on the top layer. Slide the razor down about 3/8 of an inch, then flux and bring the solder down about 1/8 " away from this. Now when you remove the razor you should have about ½ of needle from the points to the solder. When you are ready to use these, you may have to slide a clean razor or piece of paper between the layers to separate them a bit.

If you are making 9 magnums with 00 insect pins, you may need to bring the solder down a bit more to the tips.

ATTACHING NEEDLES TO THE BAR: Set the group up in the Bar jig, and place a clean Needle Bar where it goes in the jig. Make sure when you look down at the bar, that the loop, known as the eye, curls around to the left. And the needles are attached to the underside of the bar. This is just a standard so that when you set up your Machine you know the needles are riding on the tube tip just by checking the eye of the needle bar. Next flux and solder the group to the bar. The jig will make sure everything is square and nice.

Have some baking soda mixed in a cup of water handy to neutralize the flux. This can also be done when soldering machines. You can also wash your hands with the baking soda to neutralize the flux on your fingers.

•INK

•BLACK INK

Things are not like they used to be, the standard black ink in the Tattoo Industry was Pelikan "Yellow Label". Now "Yellow Label" is "Blue Label", and there is also Talenz, Sumi, and other blacks, which are manufactured by the various Tattoo Suppliers. It can become very confusing to someone getting started as a Tattoo Artist. I will explain the black inks I am familiar with. I will tell you which ones I use and what I use them for.

PELICAN: Pelikan "Yellow Label" was the standard in the industry. It use to have a yellow label, but now it has a blue label and people now call it "Blue Label". In fact a good way to tell someone who's been around a while is if they still refer to it as "Yellow Label". What ever you decide to call it, its real name is; Pelikan Drawing ink A. It also has French and German writing on the label. Pelikan is great for black and gray shading. It's the smoothest black there is. When you add water to it you can change the values, this is called "Gray Wash". I use Pelikan for all my shading, I even use it to line with if I am doing a portrait, or any other major black and gray piece that doesn't need a bold, dark outline. We used to boil it down in a double boiler to make it dark for tribal, or outlining traditional style tattoos. It's a simple process, just get yourself a double boiler, put water in the bottom part, pour the ink in the top part and simmer, uncovered, on a low to medium heat for a while.

Measure the ink level with an ice cream stick, and check it every so often. Boil off about one quarter to one third and you will have a nice dark black for outlining and tribal work. Remember if you use the boiled down ink for black and gray work, you will have to add more water to it to get the lighter values.

TALENZ: Talenz is dark black ink that I use for outlining color pieces and for tribal work. If you use Talenz there is no need to boil down your Pelikan. I don't shade with Talenz, its too dark, even if you add water to make a gray wash, it still comes out to spotty looking, like a stipple, but not in the good sense. You can completely ruin an otherwise nice black and gray piece with Talenz. I have heard of and know artists that use Talenz exclusively, they don't use any other black. I personally would not do this and recommend that you don't do it either.

SUMI: Sumi is the ink used in Japanese Sumi Ink Painting. It is made from vegetable oil or Pine resin soot, and formed into Ink Sticks that are works of art in themselves. Some Sumi Ink Sticks command very high prices and it would be unheard of to grind them down into ink. But don't fear, you can buy Sumi ink in bottles from most any Art Supply store. When you put Sumi in the skin it will lighten as it heals. So it will not heal as dark as it appears. But it heals to a beautiful silvery gray, a look you cannot get with any other black ink. If you are using Sumi for the first time do a free piece on a friend to understand how it works. Don't make a gray wash any lighter than 3:1, that's 3 parts ink to 1 part water, any lighter than this and it will completely fall out of the skin. You will have to experiment with the mix ratio yourself to find the right one for your style of tattooing. When you buy Sumi Ink make sure it is the real Sumi from an art store, be careful of what you buy from Tattoo Suppliers, the stuff some of them sell as Sumi is not real Sumi made from pine resin, its too dark, this is not to say it is no good, its just not real Sumi and will not give you the silvery look real Sumi does, which is the reason for using Sumi in the first place.

SUMMARY;

PELIKAN; Use for black and gray shading, and outlining major black and gray pieces.

TALENZ; Use for bold outlines and for tribal work.

SUMI; Use for gray specialty shading where the silvery look is desired.

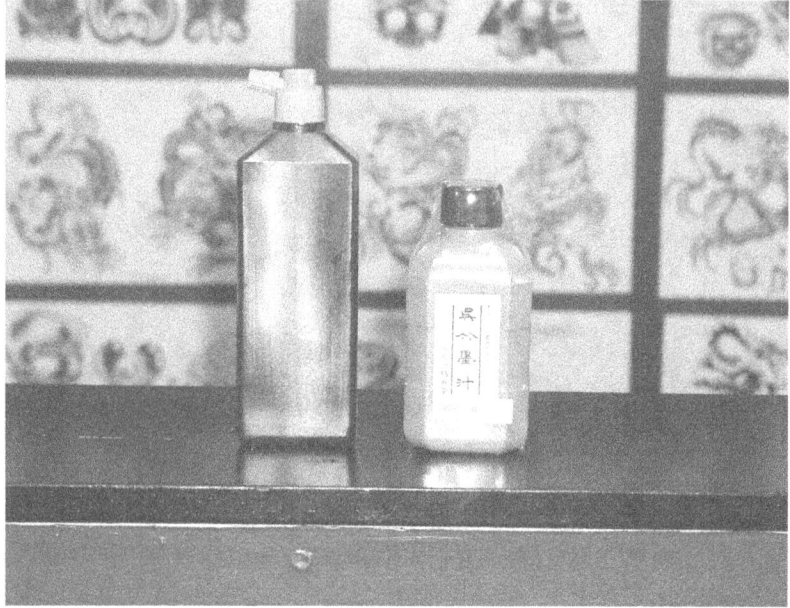

These are real Sumi Ink Bottles. If yours don't look like this they are not real Sumi Ink. The Bottle on the right is green a green container, on the left is black container with a blue cap.

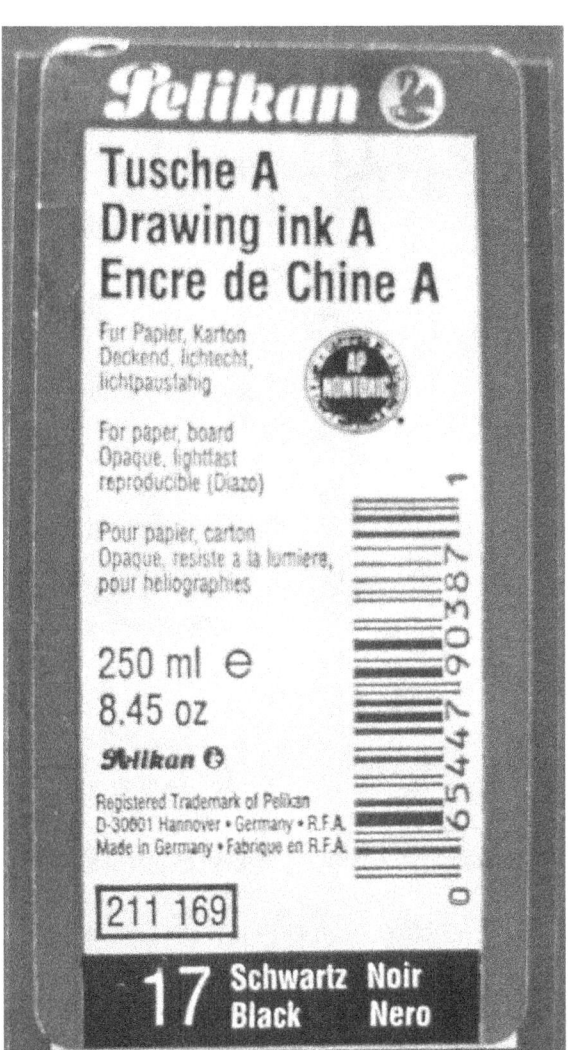

The old Yellow label.

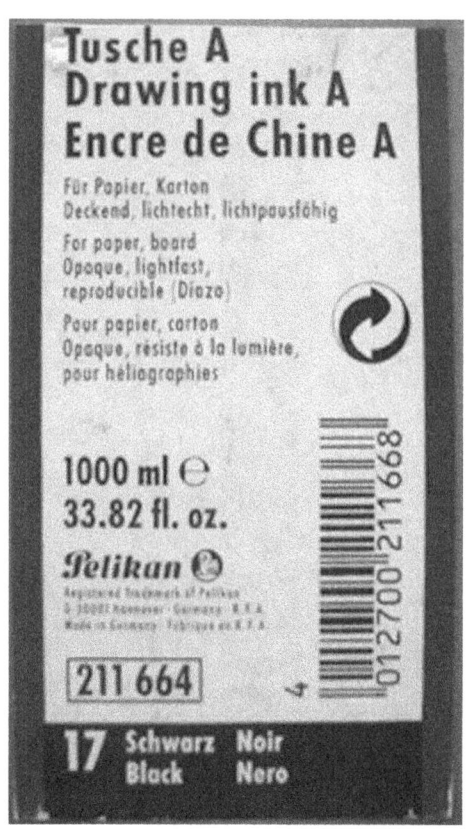

The new Blue label.

II. The Tattooing Process

•TOOLS OF THE TRADE

MACHINES: You should have at least three tattoo machines. One set up for lining and two set up for shading. Most artists I know have at least four in the shop and a dozen or more at home.

TUBES: You need at least fifteen set-ups. That's fifteen liner and fifteen shader tubes. And keep adding to this collection till you have at least thirty of each.

MAINTENANCE KIT: Get a small plastic tackle container and put in it all the extra stuff you seem to get. Washers, shims, contact files, allen keys, screws etc.

You'll also need set of metric and a set of standard Allen keys, a Phillips head screwdriver and a regular screwdriver, needle nose pliers, regular pliers, electric tape, a soldering kit, single edge razor blades, a mini screwdriver for tube grips, and a baseball bat or an axe handle.

Besides the obvious tools like Machines, power supply, tubes etc. You also need other things that are often over looked like drawing pencils, colored pencils and reference books. These are all tools just like your Machines. You should not have to borrow anything from anybody to do a tattoo. Sometimes you might have to, but some people seem to always need to borrow something everyday. If this is you, you need to take a trip to the store or call a supplier and buy whatever it is you always have to borrow. When I used to work on construction, if someone came to work without their tools they were sent home. Tattooing should not be any different.

PENCIL BOX: In your pencil box you should have your own pair of scissors, 5mil. and 7 mil tech pencils, good colored pencils like prismacolor, white out, #2 pencils, a sharpener, kneaded eraser, and I also like those white erasers that come in a click stick. You should even have a glue stick and tape. With all this stuff you wont need to borrow anything from anyone, but you can bet that you will be the universal lender. If you have to lend stuff out make sure everyone knows to put whatever they borrow back where they found it, if they cant and your stuff ends up all over the shop, cut them off. Lock your stuff up and tell them "NO". If someone doesn't like it, fuck them, they should have respect for other peoples things. Explain that your tired of finding the stuff you bought to make your work easier all over the shop, and suggest they go out and buy their own pencils.

REFERENCE BOOKS: Go to the bookstore and buy all the cool art books you can find. A good place to look is in the children's book section. I have thousands of books, most of them are art related, and the next in line are history books, they litter my home. I keep books in every room, including the bathroom. I love my books and I NEVER lend my books to any one. Well, very rarely anyway. My books help me keep my sanity, without them I would be, well, I don't know what I would be, I don't even want to think about it. I can't picture life without my books. And you should feel the same way about yours, your art books help you earn a living.

SHOP EQUIPMENT: Today's Modern Tattoo Studios have a Photocopy Machine, a Light Table and a Thermal Stencil Machine. Some Studios have Fax Machines also. And a new tool that's making its way in the Modern Studio is a Computer with good art and writing programs. A Computer is very important to have these days, along with a scanner, color printer and Internet access. With the Internet you actually have the entire world at you fingertips. When a customer says they saw something on the web, you can ask them where and pull it up for them, right on the spot. This is called service, and it's important in any type of business.

•STENCILS

Stencils used to be made by tracing over the Tattoo design on a piece of plastic. The out line of the design was scraped onto the plastic with a metal scribe. Later on Artists used an electric engraver that made life simple, almost.

Now life is real easy with the Thermal Stencil Machine. Do you remember those blue ditto copies you used to get in school, the ones that smelled real nice? The Master of those ditto copies was made with a Thermal Machine that made a Hectograph copy of the original. The Master was used as a kind of printing plate to run off dozens of copies for the kids to do their work. After they were done snorting them of course. Well anyway, someone had the ingenious idea of using that Thermal Machine to make a ditto Master of a Tattoo Design. This idea has to be the most innovative idea in Tattooing since the electric Tattoo Machine. And no one knows whose idea it was. At least everyone I asked about it. The very quality of Tattoos changed with the introduction of these new stencils into the World of Tattooing. This was the Landmark that showed a new generation of Tattoo Artists was emerging. Smarter people were learning to Tattoo, a new and better quality of Artist, along with new and better quality of Tattoos.

To make a Thermal Stencil, you have to make a photocopy of the drawing or printed outline. Some pencils will work in the stencil machine but it's easy enough to just make a photocopy. Photocopies are carbon based, and carbon is what reacts to the Thermal Master.

Take a Thermal Master and pull out the thin brown paper, this is referred to as onionskin. Some

Artists leave this onionskin in and make a stencil on it. But this doesn't mean that you have to be stupid also, pull the onionskin out.

Now cut out the design you want from the photocopy and place it face up on the yellow paper backing of the Master. Now you have the purple-coated plastic and the top tissue layer over that. Be careful not to touch the purple-coated plastic, as this is hectographic ink and gets all over the place. And if you get it on your fingers, you'll be wearing it on your nose, your ear, or any place else you have an itch. You can end up looking like Mel Gibson in Braveheart.

Now that you have your little stencil thing ready, hold it real good from the end and jab it into the stencil machine. When it comes out you will have a purple stencil on the top tissue paper. Sometimes it is a good idea to place a sheet of paper on the yellow backing, and then place the stencil copy on top of this. This will help stiffen the Master sheet, which will make it easier to jab into the Thermal Machine. Now cut out the tissue stencil along with the purple plastic under it. Discard the plastic and keep the stencil. Its also a good idea to cut around the tissue stencil once again, because the scissors tend to leave a purple border around the stencil, which can throw off your judgment when you and the client look to see if the stencil is centered on the skin.

REVERSING A STENCIL: If you have to reverse a design, make the purple stencil, then photocopy it, purple side down. The photocopy that you make from this will be a reversed image of the design. Now make a new purple stencil from this reversed photocopy. You can also use transparency film for a photocopier. Simply make a photocopy of your design on the film, and then make a photocopy of the film on paper. Since the film is clear you can copy either side. Depending on which way you want your design to face will determine which side of the film to photocopy.

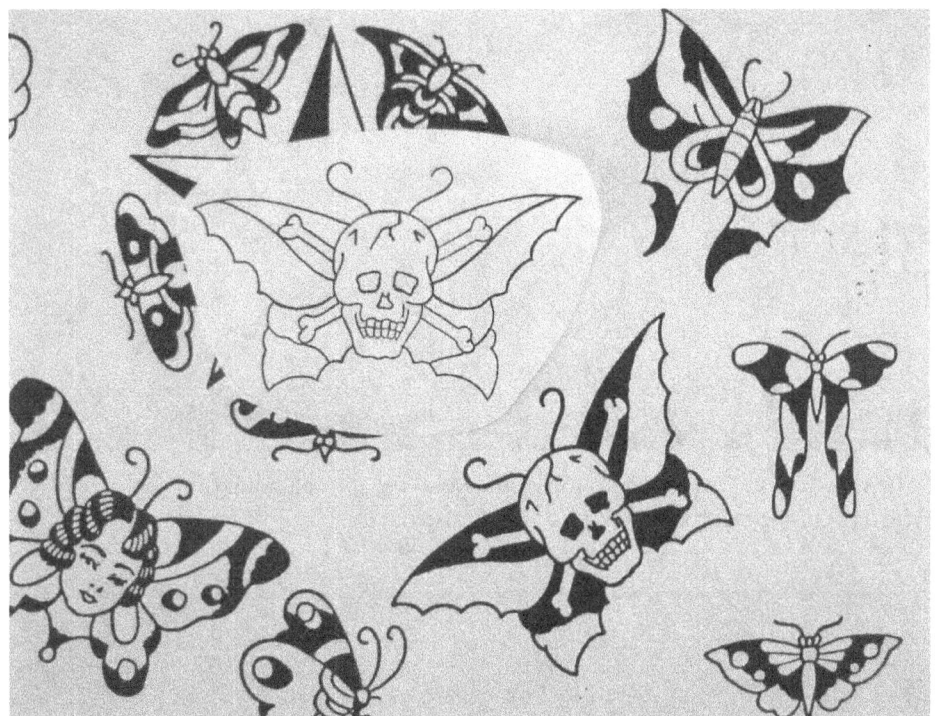

The design original and a photocopy of the stencil line drawing.

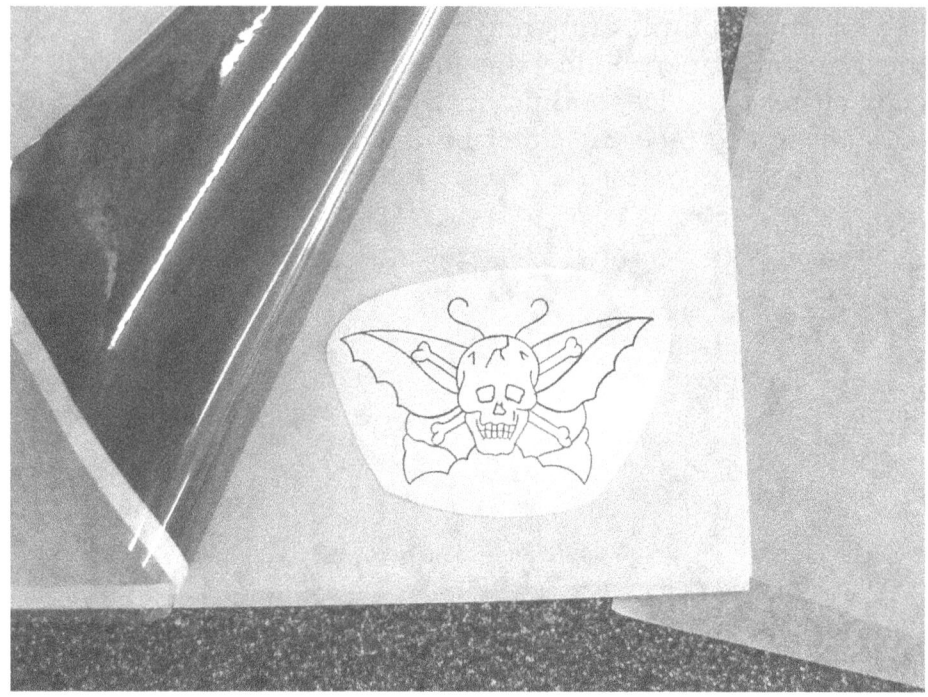

 The line drawing is placed on top of the yellow paper backing of the
Master. On the right is the onionskin discarded.

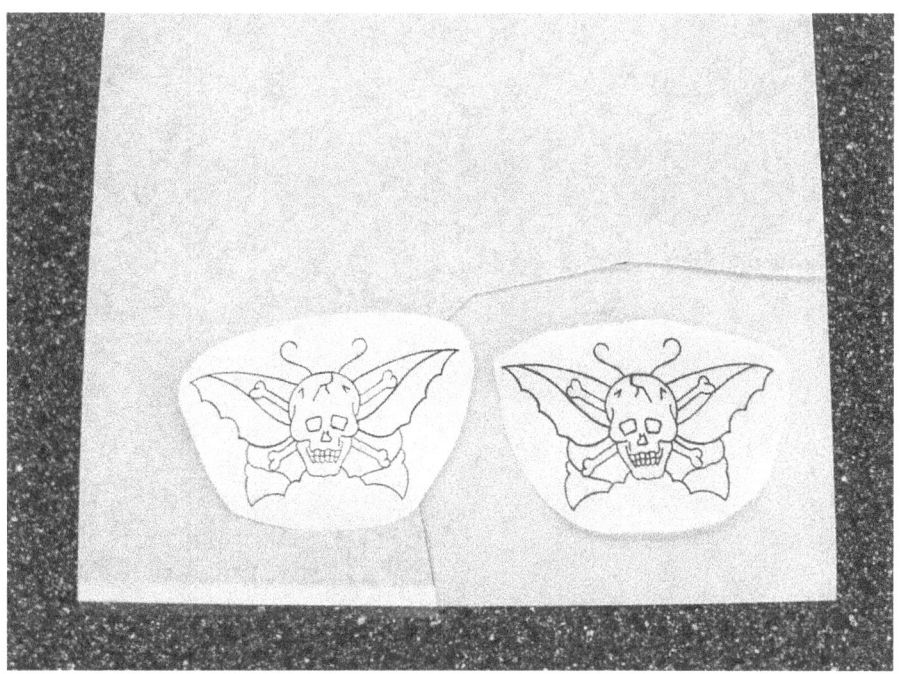

The Line Drawing (left) and Stencil (right)

• Applying the Stencil

The placement of the tattoo is very important, you can do a flawless tattoo on someone, but if it doesn't fit the area right, it will look bad. A tattoo should flow with the area; it should mimic the muscle underneath. Get a good book on human anatomy that shows muscle structure. If your tattooing someone's arm the design should always face forward. When you apply a stencil to someone's arm and they look down at it, it will look like it is too far back. Have them look in a mirror to show them that it is centered.

Before you apply the stencil to the skin, you must first prep the area. First spray the area with diluted Green Soap. Green Soap is a surgical scrub that mixes completely in water. You don't need a large soap to water ratio. All you need is about a ½ ounce to an ounce of soap in a large spray bottle, and fill the rest with water. If it suds up too much while your filling it, spray a little alcohol in to kill the suds, then finish filling. After you spray the Green Soap, shave the area. You always have to shave the area even if it looks like there is no hair. Next, spray the area with alcohol and dry it with a paper towel. Use a good quality soft paper towel as a real crappy one is like rubbing the skin with sandpaper. Now apply some Speed stick deodorant to the area and place the stencil firmly onto the skin. Apply even pressure, if the stencil is large you can grab both ends of a paper towel and press the middle of it over the stencil. Now when you peel the stencil off there will be a purple imprint of it on the skin.

If it is not positioned right you can remove it with alcohol. Sometimes it does not remove completely, but this doesn't matter, it will be light enough so it won't interfere with the placement of the new stencil.

When you and your client are satisfied with the placement, you will want to make it so the stencil won't smear and will last longer on the skin. To do this take a paper towel and lightly spray the green soap onto it to moisten it. Then press it firmly over the purple imprint. Remove it, and then do the same with a dry paper towel to dry it. Now you will find that the imprint will stay on the skin longer and won't smear while you tattooing.

You can also apply the stencil to the skin by spraying a paper towel with the green soap and moistening the area a little with this. Then apply the stencil as above. The only drawback to this method is if you have to move the stencil its almost impossible to wash off. But this method is more sanitary. There is also a sanitary way to apply the speed stick. You can scrape a little onto a tongue depressor and apply it as if you were spackling over some drywall. This way the speed stick never touches the skin and remains sanitary.

•SETTING UP THE MACHINE

The Armature pin should have a rubber nipple grommet on it to hold the needle bar in place while the Machine is running. The rubber grommets you attach directly to the needle bars suck. They don't last and it's a real pain in the ass to put them on and off every time you do a Tattoo.

Some artists work off the tips of their Machines. What this means is that they allow the needle to protrude as far out of the tube tip as possible when the Armature bar is in the down position, this is known as the Seated Position. When Lining some Artists "bury the tube", which means that the tube is adjusted, so when the Armature bar is in the Seated position, the needle hangs out to the depth that the artist wants it to penetrate the skin.

All of this is a matter of preference of the individual Artist, which can only come with experience.

MACHINE TUNING: To tune a machine you first have to decide how you want it to run. Fast and hard hitting, slow and hard, slow and soft, fast and hard, etc.
This depends on whether you are tuning a Liner or a Shader.

You should also know about Point Gap and Throw.

POINT GAP: Point Gap is the measurement between the bottom tip of the Contact Screw and the Forward Spring when the armature bar is in its seated position.

THROW: Throw is the measurement of how far the Armature moves from its top resting position to its full Seated position when it hits the top of the Front coil. This distance is measured at the Armature pin. Spring size and rear spring tension all play a role in the Throw of a Machine. Some Machines are designed with a longer frames, so the measurement from the front of the Spring Saddle to front of the Armature Bar is longer. This gives the Machine a longer Throw. This type of design makes an outstanding shader.

A fast machine always hits harder than a slow Machine. This does not mean that you cant run a machine fast and soft, it means that a fast and soft machine will hit harder than a slow and soft Machine. If you remember all my ranting about springs you know that a fast and hard Machine should have a weak rear spring and a stiff forward spring. To confuse you further, if you want a long Throw on your Machine, increase the tension on the rear spring. You can see the tension by pulling down on the armature bar with your thumb, never push down on the spring. The machine runs by a magnetic pull on the armature bar so to examine how a machine operates you need to duplicate this action. When you pull the armature bar down watch how the front spring keeps in contact with the contact screw for some of the movement. This can be adjusted by the rear spring tension. More tension will make it stay in contact longer resulting in a longer Throw. Less tension will make it lose contact sooner resulting in a Throw closer to the measurement of the Point gap.

A shorter Point gap will make the Machine run faster. Also the further forward the Armature pin is from the point gap, the longer the throw will be in comparison. If the Point gap is right above the

Armature pin, more rear spring tension will have to be used to increase the throw.

This was the logic behind the old cutback liners. The Point gap is far behind the Armature pin. With this you can have a short Point gap, which will make the Machine run faster, and a long throw for good penetration.

THE LINER: Traditionally Liners run fast and hard. With this in mind you can use it as a basis for adjusting your Machine to your own taste. The basic Point gap of a liner is the thickness of a dime. This is very basic and I don't know of anyone who adheres to this "rule". But once again you can use this as a reference point.

THE SHADER: The Traditional set up for a shader is slow and hard, with a point gap of about the thickness of a nickel. Shaders work better with a long throw. Again, this is not a rule, but can be used as a starting point when tuning your machine.

•LAYING OUT THE INK

You should have a firm cleanable surface to work from. I like to work off a piece of Glass 12"x 12". I put some non-slip drawer liner under it to help keep it in place. On this I place two layers of paper towels for my pallet when I'm ready to work. When the Tattoo is finished I just fold up the paper towels and throw the whole thing in the trash.

BLACK AND GRAY: When you lay out your ink caps for a Black and gray Tattoo take out four of five of the larger Ink caps, depending on how many different tones your going to use. Stick them down with a bit of A&D ointment. I'm left handed so I lay out my ink left to right, dark on the left, going to light. If I'm using Talenz, this would go on the extreme left, next would come the Pelikan, then the gray washes. If you follow a system like this you will always know where your dark is and where your light is. Don't laugh, it's easy to forget, they all look solid black. Unless of course if you are the Great Tattoo Master. But if this were the case you wouldn't be reading this right now anyway.

I found it a good idea not to premix your gray washes. I mix them as I need them. To do this, lay out your ink caps. Fill the first one with your straight black, the next one with, say 2/3 black, and the next with 1/3 black. You can also do this with ¾, ½ and ¼, the preference is yours. Now take a paper towel and run some water on it, squeeze a little out, and then carefully squeeze some water into the ink caps to top them off. Now you have a gradient from dark to light.

COLOR: Color is laid out the same way as the black, except usually in the smaller ink caps. And it's easier to tell the difference from dark to light.

You should usually work from dark to light when working with color. This is to stop the darker colors from seeping into the open skin and ruining the lighter colors.

You can put a darker color into the skin next to a lighter color if you put a thin layer of ointment on it, which you should be doing anyway.

•GENERAL CONSIDERATIONS

While your tattooing you should get in the habit of grabbing your spray bottle with your Machine hand, that is the hand you hold your machine in, whether you're a lefty or a righty. Call this your "clean hand". It's not going to be clean, your glove is still going to have blood and ink on it, mostly along your pinky edge. But it is going to be cleaner than your "dirty hand", the one that is stretching the skin and wiping the excess ink away. This habit will make it easier to clean your spray bottles, and any thing else you have to touch while your tattooing. This doesn't mean you can go and touch everything with your "clean hand". If you have to answer the phone or scratch an itch or something like that, remove your gloves.

You might see some artists holding the wiping paper towel in their fingers with their Machine hand. This practice goes back to when Tattooists used to use the plastic stencils. The imprint left with plastic stencils was charcoal powder on the surface of the skin, and this was easily wiped off if the Tattooist wasn't careful. So they would keep the skin stretched with one hand and tattoo and wipe with the other. This practice is no longer necessary with the hectograph stencils. Although some Old-timers still do this from force of habit, which is understandable.

If your design is going to have a background it should be opposite in texture and/or color. If the foreground is smooth, the background should be rough, and vise-versa. A darker foreground should have a lighter background. In fact, all backgrounds should be of a lighter contrast to the foreground.

You should learn the color wheel. The color wheel helps you determine contrasting colors. If you look at a blue on the color wheel the color opposite, in this case orange, would be the contrasting color. This means when these colors are placed next to each other they would both appear their brightest. You can also use the colors on either side of the contrasting color with the same effect. For some reason our brain knows contrasting colors even if we don't. If you stare at a red square for a few seconds then shut your eyes, you will see a green square on the inside of your eyelids. This is the contrasting color, and our subconscious knows it.

If you want a tattoo to look bright and colorful, its not how many colors you put into it, its what colors you put in. A tattoo of a butterfly with 3 colors, lets say blue, orange and a little light turquoise will look brighter than if you colored it in with blue, purple and red.

• TROUBLE SHOOTING MACHINES

SPITTING MACHINES: If your machines are spitting ink check your rubber bands, they might not be applying enough pressure to keep your needles in place. If they are tight enough your tube may be worn out or your needles may have been damaged while you were inserting them into your tube during set up.

Also check to see if the Needle bar is to loose or too tight on the rubber grommet. This will cause a liner or shader to spit ink.

Another thing that can cause spitting on a liner is a diamond shaped tip. If the needle isn't seated perfectly in the V bottom of the tube tip, the Machine will spit. You can fix this by using round tip liner tubes.

MACHINE NOT RUNNING: If your machine is not running at all, first check your clipcord. To do this simply hook up another Machine, if this Machine doesn't work then the problem is somewhere between the plug of your power supply and the clipcord. If it is the Machine, check to make sure nothing is grounding out at the rear binding post. If its not grounding then it must be a broken connection. Check the thin coil wires first, and then check the others. Also check the entire clipcord for defects, especially where the wire enters the spring on the clip.

ARMATURE BAR STICKING IN THE SEATED POSITION: This is definitely the wire grounding out at the front binding post.

•OUTLINING

When you outline you must hold your machine as straight up as possible so you don't blow out any lines. To blow out a line is when you go in at too much of an angle, and the line doesn't look crisp. The ink goes in at a steep angle and the line will be sharp on one side and dull on the other.

TRADITIONAL: When you outline a Traditional Old School Tattoo you should use either a 5 or a 7 Round, depending on what you prefer. Most Artists will tend to use a 7. Traditional Tattoos usually have a crisp non-calligraphied line.

NEW SCHOOL: New School is like Old School with a twist. It has the bold lines, but they are usually calligraphied. You can use either a 5 or a 7, once again depending on your preference.

FINE LINE: If you come across a Tattoo that has a fine crisp line you can use a 3 to do the outline. Fine line Tattoos should be limited to small stuff, like small roses and flowers. Don't use a Fine line to do a big Tattoo, even if the client is bent on getting a "Fine line Tattoo". Larger Tattoos look much better with a bold line, and you can calligraphy, to add interest to the design. Explain this to your client and they will usually understand, if not refuse to do the Tattoo, pass it up to someone else or send him on his way. Remember every Tattoo you do is your advertising, and people tend to remember the bad over the good.

TRIBAL: Tribal is best outlined with a 5 or a 7. It is a good idea that after the outline you fill in the pointed areas with the liner. If the tribal isn't really that big you can even color the whole thing in with the liner.

PORTRAITS: Portraits shouldn't be lined. This is not to say that you don't use a liner, but when doing a portrait its better to attack it with the shader first. Then use the liner to sharpen any hard areas. Hard, not meaning difficult, but meaning Hard edge. In fact it's a good idea to go back and forth from shader to liner to shader and so on. This way you build up the Tattoo and watch it come to life before your very eyes. You will mostly be using a shader to do a portrait though. There aren't many lines in a face, its mostly form. Clothing is where you will use the liner the most. The lines in a portrait don't really have to be fine line. In fact you will probably be using a 3 and a 5 on the same portrait.

BLOODLINES: If you're working on a Tattoo that has smoke or other negative space in it, you can use what's called a Bloodline. A Bloodline is just that, a line of blood. To make a Bloodline, dip your needle in clear water and tattoo the negative space as if you were using ink. At first you will see nothing, then you will see Bloodlines appear. These Bloodlines will stay for the duration of the tattoo. If you are working on a large Tattoo and are only doing an outline session and you need to mark the negative spaces for future sessions, you can make the Bloodline with very diluted black ink. Sumi is good for this, make a 3:1 or 2:1 mix ratio of ink to water, and line with this. It will heal very light for the next session.

CALLIGRAPHIED LINES: A Calligraphied line is a line like you see in coloring books and 1950's advertising illustration. Why Old School Tattooists didn't think of using Calligraphied lines in their Tattoo work is beyond me, and it was obviously beyond them. Now that we have more intelligent Tattoo Artists we now have Calligraphied lines. To do a Calligraphied line all you have to do is double line the spot you want thicker and fill it in with tiny circles with the liner. Or you can do the tiny circles first, and then sharpen the edges with two passes of the liner. The thicker spots look good on curves and the thin spots where one line hits another. But this is definitely not a rule and Artistic License surely comes into play here.

• SHADING

If you are shading a Tattoo that is going to be finished in color, you will only need to shade with the Pelikan black. You can also have a 3 or 5 ounce plastic cup of water set up so you can lighten the tone by dipping the tube in the water after dipping in the black. This will give you a nice feathered edge. Don't use ink caps to dip in. After a short while of Tattooing and dipping in the caps, the water will have too much ink mixed in to dilute the ink properly. A larger cup will keep the water "cleaner".

To feather an edge you have to flick the machine while pulling it off the skin. You can do this with the straight black or the watered down black.

BLACK AND GRAY: When shading for a black and gray piece, you can work from dark to light or from light to dark. With dark to light you shade in the black, feather out the edge and overlap the edge with the next lighter tone and so on.

The best way to do it though is lighter to darker. First shade out the area in the lightest tone. Then feather over the area that has to be darker with the next darker tone, and so on. If you do it this way you should use the tone in 1/3 or 1/4 increments. Start with a straight black, the next cup will be 2 parts black/1 part water. And the next cup 1 part black/2 parts water. This will give you 3 values. If you want 4 values you can divide the ink in quarters. That is 4 cups, the first being Black, the next 3:1, then 2:2, and finally 1:3. These ratios are ink to water. With a dip-cup you can lighten your mixes even further. If you are just starting out, don't use a dip-cup exclusively, use one in conjunction with the mixes. This way you have a controlled pallet of values. I set up 3 or 4 values, and a 5 or 7 ounce cup of water for dipping when I do a B&G piece. This method will give you a smooth gradient. Don't dip back and forth between the values too much, you will run the risk of darkening your lighter values. Also be careful when using this method, as it is easy to over work the skin. You may find that turning the Machine down really helps with light, subtle shading.

A good technique for shading is to shade out sideways. A lot of Artists only shade by pushing their machine forward. But, if you move the machine sideways you will get a really good effect that looks good when doing hair or feathers, and other textures also.

Remember that objects in the distance appear lighter than objects in the foreground. Also when you do a B&G tattoo use the values, have dark blacks, light grays and whites. How many B&G tattoos have you seen that are just black? Too many I'm afraid. Don't over do the white, use white only in the extreme highlights, and use it sparingly. You can also think of skin as one of your values. For example, in an eye, you will have a gray at bottom feathering lighter as you go up. Then you would have skin, then if you add highlight to the top of the "ball", the bare skin will be a value darker than the highlight

SHADING WITH COLOR: I like to call this technique "Under Painting". To do an Under Painting, you shade the tattoo in with color. For example, if you're tattooing a red rose, try shading it with a light blue, or a turquoise instead of black. Next, color the rose as you normally would. The blue or turquoise, being darker will show thru the red, and will make a really cool shading effect. Pick a color that won't over power your Top Color, but one that will add a subtle shade to it. Also don't use the Top Color's compliment as an Under Color, as this will turn to a brown when you go over it.

Here are some good color combinations:

TOP COLOR	UNDER-COLOR
Red	Turquoise/Blue/Purple
Orange	Light Purple/Red
Yellow	Red/Orange
Blue	Purple
Light Blue	Red

Whatever colors you don't see here means you should either use Gray Shading or "Scumbling" to Shade. And these colors aren't "rules" that are carved into stone, they are just suggestions.

•COLORING

DEPTH WITH SHADING: To add dimension to a color piece try shading it with gray tones first. Shade in all the shadow areas, then put the color right over the shading. Tattoo ink is semi-transparent, and the darker shading will show through, giving the piece depth. Don't shade to dark though, unless your doing a Traditional style piece.

DEPTH WITH COLOR: To show depth with color, try the "middle-tone-to-dark-tone-to-highlight" technique or what I call "Scumbling Color", because that's basically what you are doing. As a simple example, we will say your coloring a Shamrock. You will need three tones, first you will need your base color, which will be a medium tone green. Next, for your dark, use a very dark green, you may find it sold as Deep Green, it will look almost black in the ink cap. Then you will need your highlight color, which will be white or yellow, I suggest that you use white. Now, color the shamrock with the medium green, leaving the highlight section skin. Now, use the dark green, and feather it in the shadow areas right over the medium green. Because the skin is already open, it will feather in real nice and smooth. Be careful not to over work the skin. Now add the white highlight. You can even tone the white down a bit by dipping in the green first, then running the tip of your tube in the white for a few seconds, this will give your white a light tint of green.

PUTTING IN COLOR: When some one explains how to do put in color, they always say do it in tight circles. Tight circles, tight circles, I can hear them saying it right now, tight circles. Sometimes it haunts me in my sleep, tight circles, tight circles. I guess tight circles work, but tight circles are a quick way to carpel tunnel.

An easier way is to scribble the needles side to side. Try this with a tube set up in your machine, without a needle. Hold the machine like your going to tattoo your arm. Place the tip of the tube to your skin and push it forward, as if you want to scrape a groove in your arm. Try to keep the machine as straight up and down as possible, if the machine were running with ink in it, you would see straight thin lines. Try this with black next time you have to do an Indian feather or any place you need a row of thin black lines; you'll really impress your self. Now do this same "scrape a groove" thing again, but this time scribble it back and forth a little bit. Don't scribble too fast though, you will have to do it a few times too get the right feel for your style. This "scribble" technique will give you a stripe of solid color a little bit wider than the tube tip. Then you can do the same thing in reverse back over what you already did, this will insure that you got every thing filled in.

This also works well for doing solid black. If you are doing a large solid black tribal tattoo you should have a cup of water set up to rinse your needles each time before you dip back into the black. The reason for this is that as you tattoo the skin, your needles are picking up blood and other body fluids that will mix into the ink when you dip for more. This will thicken the ink and make it harder to work it into the skin. If you're ever tattooing and in the middle of the tattoo, it seems that the ink isn't going into the skin as well as it did, rinse your needles and put out another capful of fresh ink. If you are using white, you should also rinse out your tube in a clean rinse cup before redipping back into the white.

To clean the color out of the tube between colors try using an ultrasonic cleaner. You can buy a small ultrasonic from a good art supply store. There's one that has a push button on top of it, which makes it easy to turn on and off while you're tattooing. What you do is fill the tank up to the fill line with clean water, and fill a small plastic cup up with water, and place it inside the tank. Add a little soap to the cup of water, you can spray it from your spray bottle or have a squeeze bottle set up for this purpose. When you need to rinse out the color from your tube press down the little "ON" button, stick the tube tip into the plastic cup, run the machine and swirl it around for a second, and that's it! Turn the ultrasonic off and rinse the tube out under the faucet. When your finished with the tattoo get rid of the dirty cup and put a new cup about a third of the way up with water, add soap and put you dirty tubes in it and zap it in the ultrasonic for a few minutes. Then Rinse and bag them for the sterilizer.

• Bandaging the Tattoo

When you are finished with the tattoo apply a thin coat of A&D, Bacitracin or Neosporin over it. Then a clean, absorbent, non-stick bandage should be placed over it. Some Artists use plastic food wrap. While this is non-stick, it's not absorbent. Blood will start to leak from underneath it and it will look like the client is bleeding more than he really is. Dri-lok meat pads work real well, but place them printed side down, this is the side with the little holes. To hold the bandage on I use ordinary masking tape. Surgical tape sticks a little bit too good and is hard for the customer to remove, even if he wets it. Masking tape comes right off, and if it does stick too much all you have to do is wet it.

•TATTOO HEALING

This has to be the topic that Tattoo artists never agree on. You can talk with an Artist about different shading techniques or how you run your machine as compared to theirs, and they'll listen. But tell them your healing directions, and if yours don't match theirs they'll tell you your crazy!

I have heard things like; keep the bandage on for 24 hours or even for a week! Put bacitracin on it for 7 days, don't use Vaseline, and only use this kind of hand lotion. The list of stupid crap goes on and on.

So how can we figure out what the right thing to do is? First we have to figure out what type of wound a tattoo is. Yes, a tattoo is a wound. The surface of the skin was broken, blood was drawn and there is swelling.

There are five different types of wounds. They are cut, abrasion, laceration, incision and puncture. You can remember these with the acronym CALIP. A tattoo is an abrasion. I know you puncture the skin with the needles but it's not deep enough to be a puncture wound. A piercing or a bullet wound is a puncture. A tattoo is an abrasion.

How do you take care of an abrasion? If you fell off your bicycle or your skateboard and got an abrasion you wouldn't do anything, except clean it. Well, in a few hours when you get home, if you remember. That's because you didn't pay $350.00 for this abrasion. The proper way to care for an abrasion is to keep it clean and free from germs and bacteria. And to keep it uncovered so it can breathe and heal faster. The healing process should take about 10 to 14 days. Although your skin may still be healing on its own underneath, you can stop helping on the surface.

The next thing would be what type of medicine to apply? Bacitracin, Neosporin or any other antibiotic in a petroleum base works the best. It shouldn't be globbed on, too much will stop it from breathing and slow the healing process. A very thin coat should be applied; a little goes a long way. This also serves the purpose of keeping the tattoo moist. A lot of Artists will say not to use Vaseline, which is petroleum jelly, because it will suck the color out. This is ridiculous. If you read the ingredients on any of the antibiotic ointments, it will say petroleum jelly. All of them will say this, even A&D ointment. So why do some people say this will suck the color out? Because they are idiots.

If you read the directions on any of these ointments you will find that they say something like, not to use for more than a week. This is because they contain the mineral zinc oxide. Zinc will irritate the skin after a very short time. Bacitracin has the most zinc, next comes Neosporin. A&D has none because it doesn't kill germs at all. After about 4 days the skin grows a barrier layer over the wound that will keep germs out. So this is a good time to stop using the ointment. This doesn't mean you can stop caring for it. You still have to keep it clean by washing it.

We all know that a tattoo has to stay moist for about a week to 10 days, if not 2 weeks. So to keep it moist after you stop using the ointment use a good skin lotion. Once again, nothing is going to suck the color out, so it doesn't matter which one you use. A lotion with a lot of alcohol and perfume will give you an uncomfortable burning feeling on the tattoo. So its wise to use something gentle, like

108

a vitamin E lotion. Some people pop vitamin E pills on their tattoos and keep it moist with the oil. But vitamin E oil is sticky and feels uncomfortable, but it does work. Your skin will absorb vitamin E, and there is no other vitamin that is better for your skin.

Some artists say stay out of salt or chlorinated pool water, as these will suck the color out. Once again, nothing will suck the color out. If any thing, the chlorinated water will kill any germs or bacteria on your wound.

Did you ever go swimming with a cut? Then you know what happens to a waterlogged wound. It gets all gooey looking and the entire protective layer comes off. This means the healing process has to start over again. If this happens to a tattoo, you can lose color. Its not the type of water that does this, it's the prolonged exposure to water in general.

The last thing to consider is sunlight. A sunburn will screw up a tattoo. Also a tattoo is heat sensitive, you know this when you walk past a hot oven or are sitting near a campfire with a new tattoo. If your tattoo is in the sun, you will know about it because it will burn. The healing ointment you put on a tattoo will also start to fry in the sunlight, which will give you severe burns. Yes, this can and does really happen.

So from what we examined above we can come up with an intelligent set of healing instructions. You have permission to use the following instructions, as long as you use the "plug line" also. So photocopy it and hand them out to your customers.

How to care for your new Tattoo:

1- Remove bandage after the bleeding stops. Usually within an hour.
2- Wash well with soapy water; continue to wash tattoo 3 or 4 times a day.
3- Apply a thin coat of Bacitracin or Neosporin for the next 4 days.
4- After 4 days keep the tattoo moist with skin lotion or vitamin E oil for the next 10 days.
5- Keep out of Sunlight for 2 weeks.
6- Do not submerge in any kind of water for 2 weeks.
7- Do not rebandage.

Stolen from "The Art and Science of Modern Tattooing". www.moderntattooscience.com

•WASHING YOUR HANDS

Washing your hands is very important, not many people know how to wash their hands the right way. It should take you a full two minutes to wash your hands. When you wash your hands make sure you wash each individual finger, one at a time. Swirl the soap around the back and front of your hands, get in between each finger. Give it all another once over. Rinse, and then do it again. You can find literature on how to wash your hands from your local Board of Health.

• STERILIZING

Your needles should be disposed of in a sharps container after each Tattoo. Find out from your local Board of Health how they want you to dispose of a full sharps container as each county has different requirements.

Your tubes should be bagged in sterilizer pouches that have sterile indicators imprinted on them. They should be put in the sterilizer for 30 minutes at 15lbs of pressure and at a temperature of 270°. The poundage can be increased with out any problems. You can also increase the time by about 15 minutes, but the temperature should be left alone or you may find the solder melting off your tubes.

I only have to sterilize my tubes. My needles come pre-sterilized from my supplier, and I only use them once and then throw them away. To clean my tubes, I zap them in my ultrasonic cleaner for a few minutes, rinse them, double check to make sure they are shiny, and then bag them in a sterilization pouch. Each tube gets its own individual pouch. Then when I get a nice size load of tubes, they go into the Autoclave. Each area has its own regulations, you will have to check with your local Board of Health for yours. My Local Board of Health says to sterilize in individual sterilization pouches, at 270° and fifteen pounds of pressure for thirty minutes. I do it at 270° and twenty pounds of pressure for forty-five minutes. This extra five pounds of pressure and fifteen minutes of "cooking time" just adds a little peace of mind where peoples health are concerned.

III. Principles of Color

•Principles of Color

While building a telescope, Sir Isaac Newton discovered that light would break up into different colors when it passed through a prism. These colors were red, orange, yellow, green, blue, indigo, and violet. Through experimentation, scientists of the time discovered that mixing different combinations of red, blue and yellow could make all colors. These three colors they referred to as the three "Primary Colors". These studies however, were done with light rays and not with pigments. So all these experiments were not done with black or white.

In the late 1800's, Albert Munsell organized colors into a charting system that allowed us to view all the colors in the color wheel as not only pure color, but in the different values with black and white added. This charting system is known as "The Munsell System".

A scientist, by the name of Helmholz, discovered the three different dimensions of color that Munsell used to create his "Munsell System". These were Hue, Value, and Intensity.

HUE: The name of the basic color.

VALUE: How dark or light a color is. Value is achieved by mixing the Hue with black, white or gray.

CHROMA: The intensity, brightness or dullness of a color.

Colors can be Transparent, Translucent or Opaque.

TRANSPARENT: Transparent is just that, clear.

TRANSLUCENT: Semitransparent, you can see through it but some color is reflected back into your eyes.

OPAQUE: Solid color, you can't see through it at all.

Tattoo color pigment is translucent to semi-opaque, it is never fully opaque. Which means that darker colors underneath will show through the color on top.

•WHAT IS COLOR?

Color is light, without light there is no color. The color we see is actually reflected light. When light hits an object, that object soaks up the rays of light, if that object soaks up all the rays of light, we will see it as black, because no light is being reflected off and back into our eyes. If all the light were to bounce off an object we would see it as white. Some things only absorb certain light rays and reflect the others. For instance a banana absorbs all the rays of light except yellow. Yellow reflects off the banana and into our eyes, so this is the only color we see when viewing this object. So in actuality, a banana is comprised of every color, except yellow, as yellow is the only color that it doesn't absorb.

•THE COLOR WHEEL

If you look at a color wheel you will see the names of the colors, this is known as the Hue. As we already know the only colors you cant make by mixing colors together are the primary colors; red, blue and yellow. Mixing two of the primary colors together makes all the other colors in the color wheel. For example, equal parts of red and blue will give you purple. Add more blue than red and you will get blue purple. More red than blue will give you red purple.

PRIMARY COLORS: These are the three basic colors, red, blue and yellow, from which all other colors are created.

SECONDARY COLORS: These are the colors that are created when you mix two equal parts of primary colors together. These are green, orange and purple.

TERTIARY COLORS: These are the colors we create by mixing a primary and secondary color together. These colors are yellow-orange, red-orange, red-purple, blue-purple, blue-green and yellow-green.

•COLOR COMPLEMENTS

The colors directly opposite each other are complementary colors. When these colors are placed next to each other they make each other stand out. However when these colors are mixed together they gray out. This works in oil painting but not in tattooing.

Your subconscious automatically looks for a colors complement. If you stare at a solid red circle for about thirty seconds, then close your eyes, you will see a green circle on the inside of your eyelids. This works with any color. If you stare at blue, you will see orange when you shut your eyes. It's a natural phenomenon that your brain knows a colors complement and automatically looks for it, even though your conscious mind doesn't.

Tertiary colors also complement the primary colors. If you are tattooing something that is predominantly red, and you want to make it look brighter, you have a few choices. You can do some sort of background in green, but green and red next to each other may look a little to weird, as they are direct complements. So your other two choices are the Tertiary colors, blue-green or yellow-green, which would complement the red, but not over do it like green would.

ANALOGOUS COLORS: These are three colors that are right next to each other, such as green, blue-green and blue. In tattooing you really don't want to over do it with analogous colors, otherwise the tattoo will look like a blob of whatever the predominant primary color is. If you use blue and blue-green next to each other, try to complement it with orange, red-orange or yellow-orange. This will make it look bright and colorful.

Some people seem to think a colorful tattoo is one that has a lot of different colors in it. Customers will come in and ask for a colorful tattoo, with the hopes of getting seven to ten different colors crammed into that little butterfly. This is like stuffing ten pounds of shit in a five-pound bag. It is your job to explain to them that a tattoo with three colors will look more colorful than a tattoo with seven colors. Its not how many colors you use, but what colors you use.

IV. Apprentice Information

•APPRENTICESHIP

Apprenticeships can work two ways, either you find someone that wants to help you, or nobody will want to tell you anything. You should also be very careful of people that seem helpful, as they might be giving you the wrong information. Its as if they think you're going to go out and write a book about tattooing, and let everyone know "The Secrets" ;). I know that when I first started, my boss told me to put water in my ink! He gave me this "secret info" while I was working in his shop! Why do people do this? I don't know, but I have more respect for the ones that openly say they won't tell you anything, than for the ones that tell you the wrong things.

Some Tattoo Artists may be willing to teach you, but for a price. I have heard of apprentices paying up to five thousand dollars for an apprenticeship. Only to walk away with crappy equipment, and equally crappy tattoos under their belt. Some may want you to sign a contract, or some type of work agreement stating that you have to work for them for five years, and if you quit, you owe them a certain amount of money, and you cant work within a fifty mile radius or some other ridiculous crap like that. The "five years or pay" may hold up in court, but the "can't work within fifty miles" most likely won't. There is a "right to work" law, and this law protects you from these scrupulous scumbags. But if you have any doubt, show this contract to a lawyer before signing it. Or better yet, don't sign anything, find someone else to teach you. If you're a good artist on paper and have some type of personality that people like, you may be able to find someone who is willing to teach you for free, If you do find an Artist who will teach you for free, you will most likely learn more from him, than from someone trying to make a quick buck, or from one who tries to commit you to be their personal slave. But if you do find an honest person willing to teach you for free, repay him by sticking around for a while after you learn. Being a scumbag works both ways.

Advice that I can offer to the Apprentice is that you should read this book from cover to cover, and then read it again. There are also a few other books out there that you should try to get your hands on, and read a few times. Also do your first few tattoos free of charge, as you will be getting paid in experience.   After this you can start charging a modest price to help pay for your supplies. And remember the people who you "practiced" on, and when you get good, fix up those oldies you did on them! Get the people who you do your "beginner" tattoos on to sign a release form that mentions that they are aware that you are a beginner, and also include your charge for the piece, weather its free or not. This will help you avoid any legal problems that may arise.

COMFORT AND ATMOSPHERE: While it might seem good to tattoo out of your house, you will be better off trying to advance yourself and eventually seeking employment in a good studio. Most of us started at home, there is nothing wrong with this. But if you ever want to become really good you need to work in a professional atmosphere. Ask around, find a shop that does good work and has people there that you get along with. If you visit a shop and the guy you speak to is an arrogant ass, go back another day, there is always one asshole everywhere you go, you may have better luck talking with someone else on your next visit. Try getting tattooed by someone who's work you admire, talk to him or her, ask questions but don't be too pushy, and don't act like someone your not, you will get a lot further if you just be yourself, that is unless you're a jackass. This professional atmosphere is the most important asset you can have in your career. When you work in a Good professional tattoo shop, you will eat, sleep and shit tattoos. You will hopefully be tattooing everyday, so new ideas will be fresh in your mind when you start your next tattoo. At home, you most likely tattoo less frequently, so when you get a new idea for your next piece, and your next piece is three days or even a week later, the idea is no longer fresh in your mind. Like everything else Tattooing takes practice and patience, and a good, comfortable atmosphere is a must.

TATTOOS FOR BEGINNERS: Some people teaching you will insist that you do Tribal designs as the first few Tattoos, no matter what the size. I feel this is wrong, I have seen apprentices doing these large tribal designs for over five hours on people, and getting nothing out of it but frustration. When you do a tribal design, even a small one, you're never going to see your outline after it heals. You do the outline, and then cover it with black, you can't tell how good the line is. The best designs are small to medium size roses, skulls, and daggers, most of the old school stuff. In the old school designs you got everything, Good lines, black shading and color. And not a lot of detail to drive you crazy. When you do one of these designs, you can see it when it heals, and you will know what you need more practice with.

Try to stay away from thin lines in the beginning. Use five or seven liners, these are the best for the old school stuff anyway. When you have been doing these for a while and you feel confident about your lines, try using a three liner. Remember though that you will need slightly less power to push a three through the skin than you need for a five or seven. When you apply ointment to the skin don't use too much, if you do it will push the ink off the needles before they get to the skin. Only use a very small amount, a little goes a long way.

A common mistake with beginners is when they line they're too ridged. I don't know if I can explain this right, but you have to be loose when you line, more "fluid", graceful. Get in touch with your feminine side. I know, if you had a feminine side you would touch it every day. But seriously, try not to be too stiff, loosen up and flow with the lines you make.

Lettering may scare you at first but keep at it. Get yourself some font books and photocopy the fonts you want to tattoo. Some Old English, Gothic and a couple of cool Scripts. When someone wants lettering, photocopy the font, then take a piece of paper and make a straight line with a ruler. Turn it over and trace the font on the light table using the line to keep the lettering straight. If the lettering has to be curved use a compass to draw an arc. If you have to stack the letters, center them on the line you made. Don't capitalize all the letters when using script because it will look like shit. Even if the customer insists you do it, don't. Explain to them how crappy it will look and you're not going to do it. Unless of course you're doing initials and the letters are separated by periods. Another thing not to do with script is to stack it. Old English or a Gothic font looks much better when stacked.

• Lettering with a Computer

Photoshop: Open a new file. In the window that pops set the parameters to; Width 11", Height 8.5", Resolution 300 pixels/inch, Grayscale mode. Have your rulers showing (ctrl+R) if they aren't already.Press the text tool button on the tool bar, line your little cursor line thing up in the center of the window, then click. In the menu bar set the point to 72 pt and choose your font.

Type the word or saying, if you had it too close to the top and its cut off at the top, just press the move button in the tool bar and use the arrow keys to move it, or place the cursor over it and press and hold left click to drag it.

𝕭lood and 𝕳onor

This is an example of what your font should look like.

Now, press the text button again. In the menu bar you will see a button with the letter T with a curved line under it. Press it. A Warp Text window will pop. Now there are lots of cool things you can do here with this, but for this example we will be using "Arc Lower". Place your cursor on the word Arc Lower to highlight it, and click.

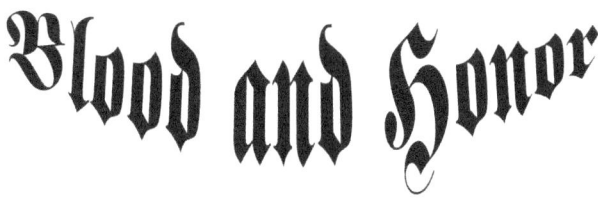

This is what you text will look like when you click the Arc Lower effect.

It looks cool like this, but lets say it is going across your client's shoulders and he wants the ends lower than the middle. So, in the Warp Text window again, check off Horizontal (it should automatically be checked) Look at the Slide Bar under Bend. Slide it over to left so it reads –25%, that's negative 25%. Or you can just type –25 in the box. When you're done click O.K.

𝕭𝖑𝖔𝖔𝖉 𝖆𝖓𝖉 𝕾𝖔𝖓𝖔𝖗

This is what you should end up with after setting the Arc Lower to –25%.

Are you ready, this is the real exciting part. Press the Move button again in the Tool Bar. Now press Ctrl+T at the same time. Now your lettering should have a box around it with a square at each corner, and in the middle of each line. If you look at the little square on the Bottom Line and put your little cursor over it, it will mysteriously turn into a small double-ended arrow. Press and hold left click to drag the square down. Drag it down a few inches. Let go of the left button, and press the Move button again. If you hold the Shift button while dragging a corner square it will keep the same proportions. Press the Apply button in the window that pops. And that's it.

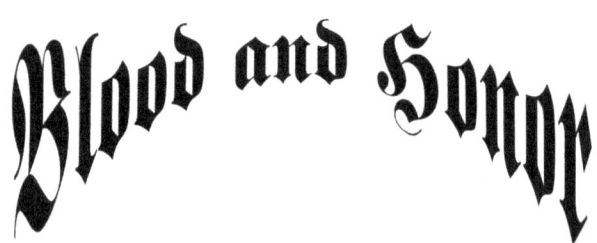

This is what you should end up with after you Apply the Transformation.

Now print it out and use your Photocopy Machine to enlarge or reduce it. You just saved a few hours if you tried to do this by hand. Experiment with the different effects, like Wave and Twist. Arc and Arch are the ones you will be using all the time.

If you make a mistake you can go to Edit→Undo or Edit→Step Backwards if you don't like something.

MS WORD: Open a new Document. Go to insert on the Menu Bar, move the cursor over Picture. In the Sub-menu that appears choose Word Art.

In the window that pops you will notice that you can do a few simple effects like Arc and Bulge. For this example we will be using Stack. Stack will be on the top row all the way on the right. Click on it, and then click O.K.

In the window that pops choose the font style you want. Choose the font point size, 36 should be good. You can enlarge or reduce it on the copy machine. Type in the word or saying you want and click O.K. When it appears you can move it around if you want with the arrow keys, or by holding left click and dragging it. You can stretch it or squash it all you want with the little squares just like in photo shop. If you hold the Shift button down while dragging a corner square it will keep the same proportions. And the yellow diamond that appears can Skew it by dragging it around. You can use Edit→Undo to reverse what you don't like.

Word is quicker and easier than Photoshop when doing simple effects like Arc or Stack. But for more complex effects Photoshop is the way to go.

KEEPING A SCRAPBOOK: Inspiration is very important in any type of art form, weather you're a writer, actor, painter or anything else. Artists find inspiration from viewing other artist's work. As Tattoo Artist we get inspired from other Tattoo Artists. This happens every time we look at a new Tattoo magazine or go to a Tattoo Convention, we ooh and aah and holy shit, every time we see a great looking tattoo. Did you ever have to do a tattoo on someone and say, "Oh, shit! I saw something like that in a magazine, let me see if I can find it", or see a great tattoo and want to achieve a similar effect in your own work? And look thru a stack of magazines, but never find it? So what I do is when I buy a Tattoo magazine, and it has a spread of an artist whose work I admire, I tear out the pages and put them into a loose-leaf binder in page protectors. This way I can ooh and aah at my leisure with out having to search thru a stack of magazines to find the picture I'm looking for.

This scrapbook isn't for copying designs directly, it's strictly for inspiration. Lets say you have to do a pin-up girl and you know in your scrapbook you stashed lots of cool pin-up chicks. You can study the way other artists did them and get an idea of how you are going to go about it. Some might say this is cheating, but it isn't. How many times have you been to the art museum and watched student painters sitting in front of a painting copying it on their canvas or sketchpad? All the time. There nothing wrong with this practice and it is completely acceptable. But remember, don't copy a tattoo directly out of the magazine, your scrapbook is there for study and inspiration only, not as a catalog of designs to show your customers. I never show my scrapbook to any customers.

RIDICULOUS TECHNIQUES: Some times people come up with ridiculous ideas to help you learn how to Tattoo. My favorite is to attach a Machine to the top of your pencil while you draw or trace a stencil. This is so you "can get used to the weight of the Machine". It sounds good but it isn't true. The Machine is closer to your hand while your tattooing so the counterbalance is different than that of a pencil. And you also have to consider that the weight of you tube acts as a counter balance, especially if your using fat grips. Another ridiculous learning technique I've come across is not allowing the apprentice to turn the paper while he is tracing a stencil, "because you cant turn your customer around". Please, turn your paper whenever you need to. It's a statement like this make us wonder how someone can be so stupid and yet still survive.

Here is another one, "Tattoo a grapefruit" to get practice. The "skin" of a grapefruit is a little bit different from the skin on a Human Being. It is not as elastic, meaning you can't stretch it, and it doesn't heal. This way you cant see what your tattoo looks like when its healed, which is more important than what it looks like when it is first done. Even the skin on a turkey or fatback is no good to tattoo on for the same reasons. It is said to do this so you can get used to the feel of the Machine. The truth of the matter is you get used to the Machine real fast, you don't need any obscure techniques to help you. Tattoo your leg, the inside of your calf. Tattoo your friends for free, you have to practice on real people.

I heard of people getting offended by saying to practice on people, as they are living humans and its wrong to use a person as a guinea pig. I even read something in a magazine where someone really verbally bashed another for asking about human "guinea pigs". But these magazines are written mostly by people who don't tattoo and probably couldn't tattoo if they tried. You need to practice on real skin, under the supervision of a good teacher. Someone teaching you should also be there watching you tattoo, not leaving you alone to figure things out for yourself. Not that they should be looking over your shoulder the whole time, though it wouldn't hurt if they did, but they should be supervising you. Even taking up the machine in their own hand to demonstrate certain techniques. Don't get your hopes up trying to find someone that will teach you this way, they are few and far between.

STRETCHING SKIN: It used to be unheard of to stretch skin between your fingers. That was because long ago Tattoo Artists used to use Acetate Stencils and Charcoal for a stencil. And the stencil would come off just by touching it. So Artists had to stretch the arm by grabbing the skin from inside the arm and pinching it. Now with the purple stencil stuff we don't have to worry about the stencil coming off, and we can touch the stencil a lot and it stays put. But its still difficult to stretch some areas, like stomachs. When a girl gets a tattoo on their stomach, you stretch it between your fingers but its still not really that tight because there is no bone or stiff muscle under it. So to make up for this you need to hang your needle out a little further than you usually do, and work off the tips.

ATTENDING SEMINARS: Seminars are a great place to pick up some real good advice. The Artists that speak at them are usually some of the top artists in the world. Some may seem a little expensive, but considering the information you get they are very much worth it. When you go to a seminar bring a notebook with you to take notes. Don't worry that you're probably the only one there with a notebook, do it anyway. No one will make fun of you, at least not to your face. But don't worry about that, you're there to learn and not taking note is like throwing your money away. Write down everything you can, ask questions, no matter how stupid you think they are. I can guarantee that any question you have, others also have, but are afraid to ask. So you will be helping a few people if you ask questions. And pay attention to other peoples questions, they may bring up some points that you haven't thought of.

V. PERTINENT INFORMATION

•BACKGROUNDS

Backgrounds should be either a complementary color or an opposite texture, or both if at all possible. If your foreground piece is mostly blue, use orange for the background, as these colors complement each other. If your going to do a gray shaded background, do it in a different texture then the foreground so it stands out. See Principles of Color for more information. Black and Gray backgrounds look good with color pieces, but a Black and Gray piece should have a Gray Wash background of a lighter value than the foreground piece. How many times have you seen Black and Gray sleeves that are just Black? Most of these are really good, artistic pieces that would otherwise look great if they had Values. So remember when thinking Background, think opposite. Of course if a B&G tattoo has a lot of dark values, the background should be light values, and vise versa.

• ETHICAL CONSIDERATIONS

MINORS: The most important ethical consideration is the Tattooing of minors. You should not tattoo any one under the age of 18. When kids are under 18 they make some pretty stupid decisions, we all know this, as we have all been there. Even as an adult we make some pretty stupid decisions sometimes. At 16 or 17 that cool taz might sound like a good idea, but at 21, well, you can see what I mean. Oh, I'm sorry, you love your taz? Yeah, sure you do. Another thing to consider is where that 16-year-old girl wants her tattoo. You can be facing sexual assault as well as other criminal charges. Where I come from, the only Tattoo shops that Tattoo minors, are the little shit shops that cant make any money otherwise.

You should always check ID without any worry about being "cool" to the teenybopper. Because when their father sees their tattoo, and they cry like a little wussbag, they'll rat you out in a heartbeat, without any concern if they are being "cool" to you. And the last thing you want is an angry father in your shop shooting off his mouth. If this happens you just may end up with assault charges also.

DRUNKS: If you think kids make horrible tattooing decisions, drunks are worse. Not to mention they smell like crap, and are belligerent and most of the time obnoxious. And they bleed a lot more, which washes down the ink. Don't tattoo drunks, explain to them that what you do is medically classified as minor skin surgery, and that they would not get drunk for a root canal.

•Diabetes

People with Diabetes should always consult their Physician before getting a tattoo. With Diabetes the immune system is weakened and people with this illness are much more prone to infection. And their tattoos also take longer to heal. So if someone with Diabetes asks you about this, tell them to talk to their doctor first. It shouldn't be a problem, but this relieves you from any legal problems. It might be a good idea to mention this in your release form.

•LIGHTHEADED AND PASSING OUT

Passing out and the feeling of being light headed is caused by a sudden drop in blood sugar. You will feel the skin of your client get cold. And his skin will be flushed out to a pale, pasty appearance. In my experience, Guys pass out more than Girls. I don't know why, and I tattoo more Girls than Guys also ;), so the odds of passing out are in the Guys favor.

Most people tell you when they are feeling sick, but some try to hide it. Another tell tale sign is that your client will yawn. If your client yawns, look immediately at his face and ask him how he is feeling. If they are sick, take a break, and offer a drink. Orange juice or apple juice is a the best remedy, as the natural sugars will help increase the blood sugar, even soda will help. You should have some juice or soda on hand for this occasion. First make sure they can have food that contains added sugar. Make sure they feel comfortable, as this is an embarrassing situation for them. Explain that this happens all the time, and its no big deal. Don't make fun of them, or try to make them look like an ass, if you do this, the only ass is you. Don't let them get up and walk unassisted, they can pass out and hurt themselves. Make sure the air conditioning is turned on, a tattoo shop should have air conditioning. You should also have smelling salts to revive someone if they do pass out. When a person passes out they sometimes go into convulsions. Everyone has their own particular thing they do. Some tighten up, some stiffen out, and some just go limp. It is your obligation to make sure they don' hurt themselves. Grab hold of them and make sure they don't fall out of the chair. A lot of people like to run to the rescue, especially if it's a pretty girl. If you need help, get one person to help you hold them down. The last thing your client needs to see is five people standing around them when they come to. These convulsions only last a few seconds and after that they just need some rest to regain their blood sugar levels. But keep your eye on them, as some people do tend to go out a second time.

Heres a good remedy that sometimes works. If your client is feeling lightheaded and gets that terrible nauseas feeling, have them lean forward in the chair. As far forward as they could, so their shoulders touch their knees. Place your hand on the back of their head and tell them to try to sit up, by pressing their head into your hand. Hold them from sitting up with your hand. Have them keep the pressure up for a few seconds. Then give in slowly and allow them to straighten up. This will force blood into their brain, and with all the oxygen their brain needs to feel better. This works about 90% of the time. However, they may still need a little rest afterwards anyway.

Hey, while I'm at it how about a cure for hiccups. Yeah, hiccups. Did you ever try to tattoo someone with the hiccups? It sucks. I once had a girl that was so nervous she got the hiccups, real bad ones, every five seconds. So this is what I did; I got a glass of water and had her hold her hands up by the side of her head, like she was surrendering. You know the "I surrender" with the hands up. Then I held the glass of water while she took a small sip. And that's it, the hiccups were cured. Her exact words were "You fixed me!" I felt like a real hero, like I just rescued her from a burning building or something.

•PREVENTING CROSS CONTAMINATION

Treat everyone as if they have a disease. This may sound cold, but as a Tattoo Artist we work on a lot of people from all walks of life. And talking to these people we know that they are not always what they seem on the outside. Someone can have AIDS or Hepatitis and not even know it. So the best prevention is to treat everyone the same. This is called "Universal Precaution", that's the official term. People like to quiz me on that. And remember it is your right to refuse service to anyone. If a Barber or Hair Stylist notices lice on a person's head, by law they are not allowed to continue the haircut. AIDS is a deadly disease, much worse than lice, so remember you have a Human Right to protect yourself from harm.

Always wear gloves before you touch some one, even if it is only to draw on them. Use the "Clean hand-Dirty hand" technique mentioned elsewhere in this book. This doesn't mean that you scratch an itch or answer the phone with your "clean hand", its just so you don't get blood all over your spray bottles and what ever else you use to do the tattoo. If you do have an itch on your nose use the back of your wrist to scratch it.

Never add fresh ink to a used ink cap if you run low on ink during a tattoo. Always remove your gloves and take out a new ink cap, and add the ink to this. And if you drop something on the floor, like an ink cap or a glove, throw it in the garbage. Don't use anything that hits the floor.

Always use new needles. The Board of Health says we are allowed to clean and sterilize, at least mine does, but we don't practice this. Most of the

Artists I know use new needles for each tattoo. Tattoo needles aren't expensive, at least when a person's health is concerned.

Don't tattoo if your mind isn't on your work. This is when you're most likely to poke yourself. If you're fatigued take a break, go to the bathroom and wash your face and hands with cold water. Get a drink, sugar also helps fatigue, so have some of that apple juice. When you go back to finish the tattoo take your time and keep your drink close by.

• COVER UPS

If you have to do a cover up, and want to design something custom to fit over the old tattoo. You need to take a tracing of the old design. Some artists like to draw on the skin. While this is very impressive to the customer, its very time consuming to the artist. Its better to take a tracing of the design.

First shave the area, then take a purple sharpie marker and carefully draw over the old tattoo. Get all the lines and mark off all the important parts that might give you difficulty, and mark off the border of where the tattoo will fit. Then when you are satisfied with your tracing, press a piece of clear contact paper over the tattoo, and when you pull it off it will lift off some of the marker with it. Stick this to a sheet of white paper and photocopy it. Now you have an exact copy so you can customize a covering design in comfort, like a Gentleman (or a Lady). You can place a clean sheet of paper over the photocopy, and draw on it over a light table.

•Accepting deposits

When you accept a deposit from a customer make sure you give him a receipt that has his name, the artists name, the amount of deposit and maybe even a close estimate of what the tattoo will cost in the end. Also make sure that you put the magic words, "NO REFUNDS", and "expires in 90 days" written clearly on the receipt. Some people don't like to hear that if they don't like the drawing they cant get a refund. Use the "Architect analogy"; "If you go to an Architect and give him a binder to draw you a house, and you don't like the house he draws, you will lose your binder. He drew the house for you, you should have looked at his portfolio before you hired him". Which is what your client should do, make sure they see some of your drawings and your tattoo portfolio. This way they will know first hand whether they like your style or not. If you end up drawing a dragon for them five or six times and they still don't like it, this means that they don't like anything. Sometimes, in a case like this, a refund or partial refund is in order to relieve you of the stress from dealing with this type of person.

•THE GOLDEN MEAN

The Ancient Greeks were one of the smartest civilizations on the face of the earth. They traveled the world, its now proven that they visited Ireland and the Americas. They were very advanced in Astronomy, they knew the world was round; this knowledge would be lost in the Dark ages with the invention of Christianity, only to be proven again by Galileo. They paved the way for the Roman Empire, and invented Mathematical formulas and ratios still used today. One of these ratios is Phi, what the Greeks called the "Golden Mean" or "Golden Section". Renaissance Artists called it the "Divine Proportion".

The Golden Mean is a proportional ratio that takes place in nature and consistently repeats itself. It's very easy to understand, and there are so many examples you can explain it forever. Watch, I'll show you, look at your finger. Look at the tip of your finger to your first joint, write the letter "A" with a pen on the first joint. Now look at the first joint to your second joint, write the letter "B" on the second joint. The distance from letter "A" to letter "B" is slightly more than one and a half times the distance from the tip of your finger to letter "A". Its 1.618 to be exact, this is the Golden Mean, 1.618. This can be found all over nature, in seashells, in leaves, trees, flowers, birds, and just about everything. The measurement isn't always 1.618, but its always close. The Greeks used this measurement in their architecture. It's pleasing to our eye, and because it's branded all over nature, our subconscious looks for it, weather we know it or not.

In the 12th century, Leonardo Fibonacci discovered a series of numbers that converge on Phi. Start with 0 and 1, now add the two numbers to give you the next number. You can continue this to infinity. Each number being the sum of the two numbers before it.

0, 1, 2, 3, 5, 8, 13, 21, 34, 55, 89, 144, 233, 377, 610, 987, 1597, etc.

If you pair two successive numbers and divide one of the numbers with the number that precedes it, the result will be very close to Phi. For example 987 divided by 610 is 1.61803..., while Phi is 1.61804.... In the beginning of the series the numbers are a little more distant from Phi. Later into the series the successive pairs approximate Phi more closely. For example, 3 divided by 2 is 1.5, and 1597 divided by 987 is 1.61803..., which is very close to Phi.

What does this have to do with tattooing? We can use it in our composition, when drawing Tribal or Biomechanical stuff. In fact when you refine your abstract drawings you probably use the Golden Mean without even knowing it. Leonardo DaVinci used the Golden Mean in his composition, and some modern Painters use it also. Frank Covino is the only Modern Master I know of that admits to using it. Many Artists use it instinctively, without even knowing it.

•Suggested Reading

•Art related books

• Drawing on the Right Side of the Brain, by Betty Edwards
This is the book to read if you think you can't draw a portrait. The part about Zen and the transitional shift is excellent.

• Harley Brown's eternal truths for every artist, by Harley Brown
This book fights for first place with "Drawing on the Right Side of the Brain".

•Drawing From Within, by Nick Meglin

•The Art of Drawing, by Willy Pogany

•Spectrum, edited by Fenner & Fenner
This has been published annually for the past eight years.

• Understanding Comics, by Scott McCloud
Understanding Comics is a course in visual psychology.

• Drawing Realistic Textures in Pencil, by J.D. Hillberry

• Complete Guide to Drawing From Life, by George Bridgman
The Fantasy Illustrator Ken Kelly first introduced me to this book when he let me borrow his copy, with strict orders not to fuck it up. I took the utmost care of it, and I enjoyed reading his personal notes in the book as much as the text itself.

•Hawthorn on Painting, by N. Hawthorn

•Controlled Painting, by Frank Covino
     Mr. Covino goes in depth about the Golden Mean.

• Also find and build a library of the following artists;
     Frank Frazetta, Ken Kelly, Simon Bisley, Patrick Woodroffe, Brom, Royo, Zook (if you can find his work), Josh Kirby, This list can go on forever, go to the bookstore or on the Internet and explore.

•**RELATED INTEREST**

     This is the indirect learning technique, like in the movie Karate Kid. It doesn't seem like your learning how to tattoo, but you will be learning things that can be applied to tattooing, and life in general.

• Zen and the Art of Motorcycle Repair, by R. Pirsig
     I was reading this book and thought it was great. I was able to relate to it, I was recently divorced, and I also have a son named Chris, just like the author. Then I made the mistake of reading the Afterword in the back of the book, which told about his sons' unfortunate death. This disturbed me very much, I put the book down and called my son, who was visiting his mother for the weekend. I never did finish reading this book, I can't read about a child who I know is no longer with us. To this day I cant get myself to finish it.

• Wooden Boat, by Michael Ruhlman
     What does building wooden boats have in common with tattooing? Absolutely nothing and just about everything.

• Sailing Alone Around the World, by Capt. J Slocum

•Hand Tools, by A. A. Watson
    There is nothing cooler than good old-fashioned woodworking tools, except maybe Antique Blacksmithing tools.

•OF INTEREST TO SHOP OWNERS AND MANAGERS:

•On the German Art of War, by Condell and Zabecki
    The principles of Military Leadership can be applied to business as well, and why not learn from the best.

•Special Men, by Dennis Foley
    This is an excellent book written by one the best American Officers. Of special interest is the intro by LT. Col. David Hackworth, ret.

•Sun Tzu and the Art of Business, by Mark McNeilly
    This book is written by an IBM strategist who is also an amateur military historian and a former military officer. In it he compares business strategies to military strategies using "The Art of War" as a backbone. Excellent comparisons to German Stormtrooper Tactics. Including military victories and blunders that apply to business as well as war.

•Words of Wisdom

"A wolf who lies in his lair never gets meat, nor a sleeping man victory."
Viking Proverb

"Losers fix the blame, winners fix the situation."
Unknown

"Obstacles are the things you see when you lose sight of your goals."
Unknown

"To all my students who taught me so much."
Nick Meglin, "Drawing from Within"

"The privilege of a lifetime is being who you are."
Joseph Campbell

"If you have no time to do something right, how will you have time to do it again?"
Unknown Boatbuilder

"The search for truth is never wrong. The only sin is to lack the courage to follow where truth leads."
David Duke

"If at first you don't succeed, try, try again."
Mickey Mouse

"Negotiations without weapons is like music without instruments."
Frederick the Great

"Courage is not the lack of fear, its what one does in the face of fear."
Patton

"Selfishness and Cowardice both travel in the same boat"

> Asatru proverb

"Men must try if they are to advance. Without effort, no one knows which way luck will turn."

> Bodvar, from "The Saga of King Hrolf Kraki"

"If you live life afraid of losing it, you've lost the idea of life itself."

> Forbes

"Poker isn't a game of cards, it's a game of people."

> Doyle Brunson

"Never interrupt your enemy when he is making a mistake."

> Napoleon

"It's a dangerous thing, walking out your front door. If you don't lead your feet, there's no telling where you'll be swept off to."

> Bilbo Baggins,
> "The Lord of the Rings"

"When two wolves fight, one is bound to be hurt, and the other is bound to die"

> Viking Proverb

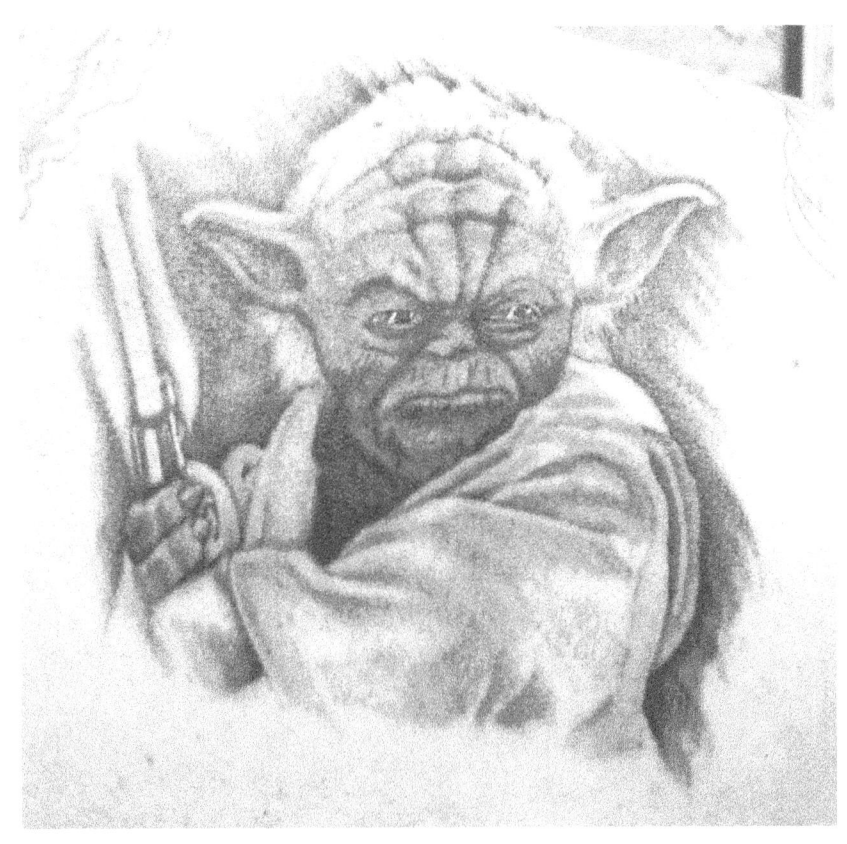

www.ingramcontent.com/pod-product-compliance
Lightning Source LLC
Chambersburg PA
CBHW081125170526
45165CB00008B/2552